RIVERSIDE CITY & COUNTY PUBLIC LIBRARY

P9-DMU-211

The Wooden Spoon Book of Home-Style Soups, Stews, Chowders, Chilis and Gumbos

BOOKS BY MARILYN M. MOORE

Baking Your Own
The Wooden Spoon Bread Book
The Wooden Spoon Dessert Book
The Wooden Spoon Book of Home-Style Soups, Stews, Chowders,
Chilis and Gumbos

The Wooden Spoon Book of Home-Style Soups, Stews, Chowders, Chilis and Gumbos

Favorite Recipes from *The Wooden Spoon Kitchen*

Marilyn M. Moore

THE ATLANTIC MONTHLY PRESS
NEW YORK

Copyright © 1992 by Marilyn M. Moore

All rights reserved. No part of this book may be reproduced in any form or by any electronic or mechanical means including information storage and retrieval systems without permission in writing from the publisher, except by a reviewer, who may quote brief passages in a review.

Published simultaneously in Canada

Printed in the United States of America

FIRST EDITION

Library of Congress Cataloging-in-Publication Data

Moore, Marilyn M.
The wooden spoon book of home-style soups, stews, chowders,
chilis and gumbos: favorite recipes from the wooden spoon kitchen
/ Marilyn M. Moore. — 1st ed.
Includes bibliographical references and index.
ISBN 0-87113-480-2
1. Soups. 2. Stews. I. Title.
TX757.M66   1992   641.8'13—dc20   92-4961

Design by Laura Hough

The Atlantic Monthly Press
19 Union Square West
New York, NY 10003

For Shirley, Joe and Linden,

who grew up on my soups

Acknowledgments

Heartfelt thanks to those who shared recipes with me: Harry Dyck, Martha Mervis, Selma Young.

Thanks again to my intrepid tasters, who tasted everything I put in front of them and did not hesitate when their bowls were filled with hot chili on a 95-degree day. At the library: Lou Graham, Evelyn Hartz, Carol Arnold, Maria Smith, Scarlet Cropper, Donna Judy, Ruth Neathery. At Flowers and Gifts by Molly Culbert: Molly and James Culbert, Louise Barten, Evelyn Brown, Judy Custer, Joanne Elliott, Laura Hathaway, Darlene Van Pelt, Pat Regan, Martha Zamarripa.

A sincere thank you to Karen Tracey of the USDA Food Safety and Inspection Service toll-free hotline (800-535-4555) for answering my questions about food safety in the making of soups.

My agent, Elise Simon Goodman, has the solutions to all my problems. Thank you, Elise, for being everywhere at once.

Every food writer has a composite idea of what a cookbook editor should be. Mardee Haidin Regan is that editor. Thank you, Mardee, for being the best.

Contents

Contents

Hearty Soups
With meats, pasta, grains or legumes
Curried Quinoa-Tomato Soup   Vegetable Barley Soup
Turkey Noodle Soup with Old-Fashioned Egg Noodles   Alphabet Soup
Mulligatawny with Raisin-Rice Pilaf   Spaghetti Sauce Soup
Italian Sausage Soup   Martha's Sweet-and-Sour Cabbage Soup
Ukrainian Borsch   Oxtail Barley Soup   K.C. Steak Soup
Ham Vegetable Soup   Poor Man's Bouillabaisse   Selma's Lentil Soup
Fruited Lentil and Rice Soup   Beer Garden Pea Soup   Hoppin' John Soup
Black Bean Soup   Basque Bean Soup
Ham and White Bean Soup   Yellow Pea Soup

Savory Stews
With stick-to-your-ribs goodness
Ratatouille   My Easy Minestrone   Moore's Meatless Minestrone
Polish Bigos   Pork and Potato Stew   Porcupine Stew
Savory Beef Stew   Old-Fashioned Beef Stew   Yogurt-Beef Stroganoff
Hungarian Goulash   Stacked Irish Stew   Lamb Stew with Apricots
Brunswick Stew   Chicken Stew with Peas and Mushrooms
Chicken Stew with Butter-Biscuit Dumplings

Chunky Chowders
Thick and delicious
Country Corn Chowder   Deutsch Ham Chowder
Bean and Bacon Chowder   Cheeseburger Chowder
White Clam Chowder (New England-Style)
Red Clam Chowder (Manhattan-Style)
Salmon Chowder   Tuna Chowder   Tuna-Cheese Chowder
Corn and Tuna Chowder   Succotash Chowder
Parsnip Chowder   Broccoli-Cauliflower Chowder   Potato Chowder

Introduction

Soon after I finished my last book, I began asking groups I teach to help me choose a topic for my next. I gave them several alternatives and they resoundingly chose soup. I agree with their choice.

But what kind of soup book? I decided to write a down-to-earth book with recipes for unpretentious food. The kind of food that I like to serve to my friends and family, made from recipes you can use without taking a culinary course.

All of these recipes can be made in a reasonable amount of time. Everyone is so busy these days. Of course, you want to know how to make a good pot of stock, in case you get snowed in some weekend and the urge to "really" cook comes over you. Stocks can also be made in a pressure cooker (see page 14). But you can make good soup without having to make a pot of stock first. Recipes that require stock list canned broths as alternatives. Some soups can be made with either stock or water. Many require no stock at all.

These recipes have good old-fashioned flavor. They don't rely heavily on butter, cream or other fats to get that flavor, but those ingredients are used in moderation when I feel they are needed. Although this is not a diet book, the recipes lean more toward the use of fruits, vegetables and complex carbohydrates and less toward the use of meats. The fats I use are chosen with care. Canola and olive oils are the oils of choice because of their chemical properties in relation to cholesterol. Butter is used in moderation, however, and is considered good food that can be included in a healthful diet. For the cook who wishes to avoid butter, there are many recipes to choose from.

I specify lowfat milk products when they work as well as their high-fat counterparts, but do not hesitate to call for small quantities of butter or cream or if their inclusion is needed for the success of the dish. Lowfat cheeses often are substituted for higher-fat types, but if this results in a compromise in flavor, I retain the higher-fat version. I realize this is a dichotomy, but it is the way I cook and eat—mostly, with a spartan hand; now and then, with indulgence. Those who are on a restrictive diet and those who are not should be able to find here tasty recipes they want to try.

I am a strong advocate for the use of fresh herbs rather than dried and suggest ways that you can easily grow your own, in the garden or on a windowsill. For the cook who does not wish to garden, there are guidelines for converting fresh quantities to dried, particularly for herbs not normally available fresh at the market.

We all know that soup is good for us—our mothers told us that for years. There is also evidence to prove that eating soup can help with a weight-loss diet. In a study conducted by University of Pennsylvania researchers, it was shown that soup taken at the beginning of a meal slows the rate of eating, resulting in lower calorie consumption overall.* I can report that this is the first cookbook I have written during which I have managed to lose rather than gain weight in the process. So, enjoy! I certainly have.

MARILYN M. MOORE

*This study was conducted by Henry A. Jordan, M.D.; Leonard S. Levitz, Ph. D.; Karen L. Utgoff, M.B.A. and Hau L. Lee, M. Sc. and was supported by a grant from the Campbell Soup Company. It was reported to the American Society of Bariatric Physicians meeting at Las Vegas, Nevada, in October 1979.

Everything You Ever Wanted to Know About Making Soups

The Right Equipment

Choosing a few simple pieces

Making soup does not require a lot of special equipment. If you've been cooking for a while, you won't need to shop before making your first pot of soup. If you're just starting out or updating what you have, read on before buying.

Can opener and corkscrew   Don't forget you'll need a corkscrew to open wine (and some vinegar) bottles, and it's impossible to go very long without a can opener.

Colander   This is useful for draining the water from washed vegetables and fruits. It can also be lined with cheesecloth and used for straining in the absence of a sieve.

Cutting board   Plastic and resin cutting boards are more sanitary than wood. Keep your board washed and rinsed after each use. Because of the prevalence of salmonella contamination in the domestic fowl population, one should never cut chicken or other fowl on a wooden board. After using any board for cutting fowl, wash well with soap and rinse and dry before using for anything else.

Dutch oven   A dutch oven or large-capacity, stovetop-to-oven casserole is desirable for making some of the oven-cooked stews.

Food mill   A food mill is an inexpensive, nonelectric piece of equipment. It has a rotating blade (you and your arm provide the rotation) that presses the soft part of foods through a perforated disk, leaving the fibers behind.

Food processor and blender   A food processor will grate, chop, slice, puree and mix most anything. It will even knead bread dough. For small amounts of vegetables and fruits, you may find it easier to use a mini version or a knife and cutting board, but for large quantities, a full-size food processor is a real cook-saver. Food processors are excellent for grinding beef, as you can control the grind from coarse to fine. Simply cube the beef or buy already cubed stew meat. Process with the metal blade until the desired grind is reached. The same method can be used to make ground pork or poultry. A blender will not replace a food processor, but it can be used to produce a smooth puree. Consider the new immersion-type, stick blenders for pureeing a soup right in the pot on stovetop.

Grater   An old-fashioned standing box grater will take care of any grating, from potatoes to citrus zest. Use it any time you don't want to enlist the aid of a food processor.

Knives   High-carbon stainless-steel knives are highly recommended and easy to keep sharp on a whetstone. An 8- or 10-inch chef's knife and a small paring knife are all any cook really needs. I forsake the paring knife and use my smaller chef's knife as an all-purpose tool. It saves the time it takes to put one tool down and pick the other up. The metal extension of a chef's knife blade should continue through the length of the handle and be riveted in place (called full-tang construction).

Ladles   Ladles are helpful in transferring soups from pot to serving bowl. My favorite ladle is of single-piece, stainless-steel construction with a 3¼-inch bowl and a 13-inch-long handle. It has a 4-ounce capacity.

Lemon zester   This small tool removes just the outer, colored layer of skin from citrus fruits (the zest), leaving the bitter part behind.

Measuring spoons and cups   In stainless steel you need spoons measuring ⅛ teaspoon (sometimes hard to find), ¼ teaspoon, ½ teaspoon, 1 teaspoon, ½ tablespoon and 1 tablespoon. Also in stainless steel look for cups measuring ⅛ cup (sometimes hard to find), ¼ cup, ⅓ cup, ½ cup and 1 cup. In glass you need cups with pouring spouts and gradations marked on their sides measuring 1 cup, 2 cups and 4 cups. Despite the ubiquity of plastic, I prefer stainless steel and glass.

Microwave oven   I am not attuned to cooking with a microwave, and I fail to see where it would be an advantage in the making of soups. The precision with which one must use the appliance puts a damper on creativity, and a microwave often takes as long as a stovetop when large quantities are involved. It does, however, do a marvelous job of reheating single servings, and can be used as an alternative to stovetop in any recipe steps you wish.

Nonstick skillet   A nonstick skillet enables you to sauté with little or no added fat. Look for sturdy pan and handle construction.

Peppermill   Essential for freshly grated pepper. Buy one that allows you to adjust the coarseness of the grind.

Potato or vegetable peeler   An inexpensive, stainless-steel (or carbon-steel) peeler will help pare potatoes and other vegetables, but it's not essential if you're adept with a knife.

Pressure cooker   A pressure cooker can speed the cooking of stocks (see page 14). I prefer not to use it for cooking the soups themselves as the compressed cooking time can produce an overcooked mixture in a hurry.

Saucepans   One 3-quart saucepan will take care of all the small-recipe soups in this book. Other desirable sizes are 1-quart and 2-quart. I prefer stainless steel with copper or aluminum inlaid or clad on the bottom for even distribution of heat, because it is nonreactive in the presence of acidic foods. Foods cooked in stainless steel can also be refrigerated without transfer to another container. It's desirable that the largest saucepan have a loop handle on the side opposite the long one, making it easier to move the pot when full.

Serving cups and bowls   Different soups call for different serving dishes. Small cups and bowls made of delicate china or glass are appropriate for appetizer or dessert soups. Larger bowls, both deep and shallow, can be used for main-course soups. Soup plates with flat rims are perfect for chowders or any soup with chunky ingredients. Mugs and individual casseroles add variety to presentation. Let your friends and family know you have added some of these to your birthday and other wish lists. Before long, you may have quite a collection.

Sieves and strainers It's nice to have an assortment, but one medium-mesh strainer will do. Buy an attractive one and hang it near the sink. Although most often used to strain liquids as you pour from the pot, it can also be used in the pot itself. Push it down into your soup or stock and the strained liquid will flow into the bowl of the strainer. This makes it easy to ladle out what you want without interference from the solids in the pot.

Skimmer This is a flat spoon with a fine mesh or finely perforated bowl for skimming foam from soups or stocks.

Slotted spoon This is a long-handled spoon with slots or holes in the bowl for removing solids from soup or stock, while leaving the liquid behind.

Stockpots These are bulky items and your final choices may depend on available kitchen or pantry storage space. A medium-size stockpot, 5 to 6 quarts, will handle any of the stocks or large-recipe soups in this book. I prefer stainless steel with copper or aluminum inlaid or clad on the bottom for even distribution of heat. Some of the newer anodized aluminum pots (which the manufacturer states will not oxidize on contact with acidic foods) are fine for cooking, but I feel safest going from stovetop to refrigerator in stainless steel. A good stockpot will be taller than it is wide, allowing for perfect simmering with minimal evaporation. A dutch-oven shape, wider than it is tall, is not as desirable for stovetop cooking. A stockpot is an expensive investment, but a good one can last a lifetime. Don't buy a lightweight stockpot just because it is cheap. Stock is heavy and a stockpot must be of heavy construction to hold it. Take your time in shopping and watch for periodic sales.

Timer   If you are as forgetful as I, you need a timer. If you leave the kitchen to do other things while the pot simmers, get one that can hang on a cord around your neck or clip onto a pocket or belt.

Tureen   A tureen is a lovely extravagance. You can always serve soup from a pot in the kitchen, but ladling from a tureen makes everything so much more festive.

Wire whisk   This is a useful tool for whipping ingredients together and for smoothing a sauce that threatens to lump. The best whisk is made of stainless steel with a comfortably thick, well-sealed handle. Look for a sauce whisk, which is more slender than the plump balloon type. An ideal length is 12 to 14 inches.

Wooden spoon   I use a rounded wooden spoon for general mixing and find that a straight-edge wooden spoon is perfect for stirring on the stove. The straight-edge tool has a nearly flat front edge, making it as much a scraper as a spoon—a boon for scraping browned bits of meat and vegetables from a sauté. Look for a good, heavy-weight, well-finished spoon made from a hardwood.

Selecting and Storing Ingredients

What to look for and what to do with it when you get it

Fresh, fresh, fresh. I can't say it often enough. Fresh fruits, vegetables and herbs are the ingredients of outstanding soups. Here are some tips for selecting the best and knowing how to care for them when they are yours.

Apples   Look for well-shaped fruit with ripened color. Avoid soft or bruised fruit. Can be stored in plastic bags in the refrigerator crisper for 1 to 2 weeks.

Asparagus   Choose tender, straight, green stalks. Avoid spreading tips or woody stems. Can be stored in plastic bags in the refrigerator crisper for 1 to 3 days.

Green beans   Search out smooth crisp pods, well filled with immature seeds. Avoid limp, wrinkled or fat overmature pods. Can be stored in plastic bags in the refrigerator crisper for 1 to 3 days.

Blueberries   Select plump berries with a deep blue color. Can be stored in the refrigerator in moisture-proof wrapping for 1 to 2 days.

Broccoli   Look for dark green heads with tightly closed buds. Stalks should be tender yet firm and leaves should be fresh and unwilted. Avoid yellowed buds or rubbery stems. Can be stored in plastic bags in the refrigerator crisper for 2 to 4 days.

Cabbage Choose heads that are solid and heavy for their size. Avoid heads with splits or yellowed leaves. Can be stored in plastic bags in the refrigerator crisper for 3 to 7 days.

Carrots Choose well-shaped, firm, bright-orange carrots. Avoid those with splits or blemishes. If there are greens attached, they should be fresh, not wilted. Remove greens before storage. Can be stored unwashed in a perforated plastic bag in the refrigerator crisper for 1 to 4 weeks.

Cauliflower Select firm, compact heads with white florets and bright green leaves. Heads with black or brown spots should be avoided. Can be stored in plastic bags in the refrigerator crisper for 2 to 4 days.

Celery Choose a firm bunch with crisp stalks. Leaves should be light or medium green. Avoid limp stalks or yellowed leaves. Can be stored in a plastic bag in the refrigerator crisper for 1 week.

Corn Look for bright green, snug husks covering firm, milky kernels. Buy soon after picking and cook as quickly as possible. Cleaned corn can be stored in plastic bags on a refrigerator shelf for up to 24 hours.

Cucumbers Select crisp, firm, bright-green cucumbers. Avoid soft or yellow ones. Can be stored in plastic bags in the refrigerator crisper for 1 week.

Garlic Choose large heads with full cloves. They should be firm, not dry and papery. Store in a cool, dry place.

Herbs Fresh herbs are so colorful and alive with flavor. Don't substitute the dried unless you simply can't get fresh. The best way to have them on hand is to grow them yourself. They can be grown out-of-doors in the summer, either in pots or in the ground. If in pots, they can be brought in when the weather cools in the fall, to grow through the winter indoors. If they are grown in the ground, the plants can be lifted to pot. If the plants are too large to lift, cuttings can be rooted for potting later. Simply cut tender stems that are 2 to 4 inches long; remove the bottom set of leaves from the stem; dip each cut stem in rooting hormone powder; stick the stems in moistened soilless mix; water sparingly and watch for new growth to appear. Remove the rooted cuttings and transplant to pots. Basil cuttings root easily in water and may either be grown in that medium or potted in soil after rooting. The first varieties to grow for your soups are: basil, chives, dill, marjoram, oregano, curly parsley, Italian parsley, rosemary, sage, summer savory, tarragon, thyme and lemon thyme. If you need further help to keep your thumb green, I recommend *The Garden Primer* by Barbara Damrosch. To substitute dried herbs for fresh, use only one-third to one-half of the required fresh quantity.

Mushrooms Cultivated mushrooms should be firm and white and relatively clean. Avoid any dark, bruised ones. Can be stored unwashed, loosely covered, on a refrigerator shelf for 4 to 6 days.

Okra Choose tender, bright green pods. Avoid overmature pods as they tend to be woody—if you can't easily slice it, you don't want it. Can be stored in plastic bags in the refrigerator for 1 to 2 days.

Onions Buy onions in mesh bags. Select those which do not appear ready to sprout. They should be stored in a cool, dry place, but not in the refrigerator. Place the mesh bag inside a paper sack to contain the debris that forms as the onions shed their skins. If you grow your own onions, they should be pulled up after the tops have fallen. They need to be spread out in a warm, dry place on paper to cure for several days. They then can be braided together, with some twine added to the braid for strength, and the braids can be hung in a cool, dry place. Simply cut off the bottom onion to use as needed. They will keep for several months.

Parsnips Choose young, straight firm roots without blemish. Avoid large roots—they tend to be woody. Can be stored unwashed in perforated plastic bags in the refrigerator for 1 week.

Sweet bell peppers Fresh bell peppers are firm and well-shaped with a shiny flesh. They come in green, yellow and red as well as other, more exotic, colors. Avoid limp, soft or wrinkled peppers. Can be stored in plastic bags in the refrigerator crisper for 4 to 5 days.

Plums Plums should be plump and smooth, firm but not hard. Avoid cracked or softened fruit. Can be stored in plastic bags in the refrigerator for 1 week.

Potatoes   The favored potato for soup is the white or russet potato. Older potatoes will thicken soups more than younger ones. Choose firm, uniform potatoes, free of cuts, sprouts or decay. They should be stored in a cool, dry place, away from sunlight. Potatoes that are exposed to the sun may develop green skin areas. These contain alkaloids, which are poisonous. Peeling a slightly green potato deeply should make it safe to eat. Potato sprouts also contain alkaloids and should be removed before potatoes are cooked.* Storage time depends on the type of potato and the season of the year, but most will keep for 2 weeks at room temperature. New or red potatoes, also known as waxy potatoes, are best soon after harvest. Select fresh-looking uniform tubers and use them soon after purchase. They will hold their shape better than the mealy white potato and will not thicken the soups when added.

Rhubarb   Select firm crisp stalks with bright red color. Avoid wilted or oversize stalks. Can be stored in plastic bags in the refrigerator for 1 to 3 days.

Scallions   Scallions or green onions should have firm white bulbs with crisp green tops. Avoid those with withered or yellowed tops. Can be stored in plastic bags in the refrigerator crisper for 2 to 3 days.

Shallots   Choose firm, well-shaped bulbs that are heavy for their size. The papery skins should be dry and shiny. Store in a dark, cool, dry place. They will keep for several months.

Summer squash   Squash should be firm and tender with fully developed color. Avoid those that are bruised or soft. Can be stored unwashed in perforated plastic bags in the refrigerator for 3 to 4 days.

Strawberries   Select berries that are bright, plump and solid in color with stems attached. Use as soon as possible. Can be stored unwashed in the refrigerator for 1 to 3 days.

*Harold McGee. *On Food and Cooking: The Science and Lore of the Kitchen*. New York: Scribner's, 1984, p. 159.

Tomatoes Tomatoes should be vine-ripened and fully colored. Slightly underripe fruit can be ripened on the kitchen counter. Ripe fruit can be stored in the refrigerator for 2 to 3 days, but flavor is best in tomatoes that are stored at room temperature.

Turnips Choose small, firm, slightly rounded turnips. Avoid large ones as they tend to be strong-flavored and woody. Can be stored unwashed in a perforated plastic bag in the refrigerator for 1 week.

Wonderful Beginnings

Making homemade stocks, when you feel like cooking from scratch

Stock is a nourishing liquid made from the slow and long simmering of meats and/or vegetables to extract the nutrients and essential flavors of the ingredients used. It forms the basis for your best soupmaking efforts.

Ingredients for stocks   Resist the temptation to empty the week's leftovers into the stockpot with a few quarts of water, expecting the whole mess to turn into beautiful stock. Indiscriminate dumping of the refrigerator's contents will result in an unsightly liquid with unappealing flavor. If you're going to take the time to make stock, start with good ingredients.

Good doesn't mean extravagant. Meats for stockmaking include some of the least expensive cuts. A meaty soup bone or a package of chicken backs and wings is very economical. Fresh meats can be combined with cooked meaty bones or poultry carcasses, and indeed, excellent stock can be made from the carcasses of cooked poultry alone. The three aromatic vegetables that form the basis of most stocks are on hand in most kitchens: onions, carrots and celery. Beyond those, just a few sprigs of parsley with perhaps some leafy herbs and spices are all that are needed to season the pot.

Preparing the ingredients   Beef can be used as it comes from the supermarket package. Chicken, however, should be washed under cool running water before adding it to the pot. Vegetables need only be scrubbed well—peels can stay on, unless the recipe says otherwise. Onion skins help give stocks a rich color. The carrots, celery, onions and other vegetables used in stocks should be only coarsely chopped. The cooking time will be lengthy and you don't want the vegetables to cook to a puree. Avoid using strong tasting vegetables, such as broccoli or cabbage, as they produce unpleasant flavors when cooked for a long period. Parsley and other herbs are used as sprigs or branches as these can easily be strained from the pot when the stock is done.

Cooking the stock   Avoid aluminum pots because uncoated aluminum can and will react with certain acidic ingredients—wine, tomatoes, lemon juice, etc.—changing a food's color and flavor. Stainless steel is my preferred choice. (See a further discussion of choosing a stockpot in "The Right Equipment," page 6.)

Always start stock with cool water. As you cook the stock, the heat will slowly raise the temperature of the water until the kettleful is gently simmering. It is the long, gentle simmering that extracts the flavors of the stock ingredients, leaving a liquid that has a pleasing clean-cut character. If the slow simmer creeps into a boil, the liquid may become clouded with particles suspended in the broth. By keeping the lid slightly ajar you can prevent the undesirable heat build up and produce a clearer stock.

Pressure-cooking stocks   You don't need to run out and buy a pressure cooker, but if you already have one, it can come in handy for making stocks in a fraction of the time required by the usual method. Prepare the ingredients just as you would for a stockpot. Fill the pressure cooker no more than one-half to two-thirds full. (Check the manual that came with your pressure cooker for specific recommendations.) Make sure that all the solid ingredients are covered with liquid. If the pot is too full, divide the recipe in half. Divide the time required to make stock by the slow simmering method by one hour. Multiply that figure by 10 minutes and pressure-cook your stock for that time. For example, if a stock is supposed to simmer for 4 hours, you will pressure-cook for 40 minutes (4 hours divided by 1 hour = 4; 4 times 10 minutes = 40 minutes).

Straining the stock   For most soups, straining the stock through a sieve is all that is needed. If the simmering process has indeed been gentle, your stock should have a healthy look that is not unduly cloudy. If you prefer more clarity, you can strain the stock a second time through several layers of dampened cheesecloth. But to clarify a stock with egg whites? I never do. And there is no reason to do so for any of the recipes in this book. There are several sources that describe the process. If you wish to try it, I refer you to *Larousse Gastronomique* for a classical explanation.

Cooling the stock   You want to cool the stock quickly. If you simply put the whole quantity of stock in one container in the refrigerator, the outermost stock will chill, while the center remains hot, and the stock may sour. As soon as the stock has been strained, pour it into quart-size containers, as these will cool more quickly than the whole potful. Stand the quarts of stock in a sinkful of cool water. Change the water once or twice, if needed, to cool the stock to room temperature. Cover the cooled stock and refrigerate. There is no need to remove the fat from the stock before refrigeration, as it will help to seal the stock while in storage.

Storing the stock   Stock can be stored in a refrigerator for up to 3 days. If you wish to refrigerate it for a longer period, discard the fat that has solidified on the surface, bring the stock to a gentle boil and repeat the cooling process. Stocks may be frozen after thorough chilling in the refrigerator. To save freezer room, strained stocks can be boiled, uncovered, until reduced to half or less of their previous volume. Freeze in quart-size freezer containers, leaving 1 inch of headspace for expansion. Alternately, freeze in ice cube trays. Frozen cubes of stock can be transferred to plastic freezer bags for storage. Reduced stocks can be reconstituted with water after thawing. If a stock was weak before reduction, you may not want to reconstitute fully. Let your taste be your guide. Frozen stocks can be stored for up to 3 months.

Stocking the Pantry

For making impromptu soups

It's nice to have a few things on hand for soupmaking, so that you can throw together a kettle or two without having to go to the market. Keep some basic canned broths on hand at all times for making soup when you don't have the time or the inclination to make stock. I have added other items that I think will assist in your soup repertoire.

Canned broths Taste what you have available and choose a brand you like, and then buy multiple cans that contain about 2 cups. Manufacturers have been downsizing canned broths; yours may be anywhere from 13 to 16 ounces. Use 1 can for each 2 cups of stock called for, adding water to make up the difference. Low-sodium broths are best because you can add salt, if desired, but you can't take it away. Store both chicken and beef varieties.

Canned tomatoes Find a brand you like and buy multiple cans that contain about 2 cups (can sizes will vary).

Tomato sauce Eight-ounce cans of unseasoned tomato sauce offer the most versatility.

Canned beans When you are in a hurry for bean soup, use cans of kidney beans, navy beans, pinto beans and black or turtle beans. One 16-ounce can is the equivalent of 2 cups of home-cooked beans.

Dried herbs Not all garden herbs can be successfully replaced by dried. Of the ones that can, I suggest you stock thyme, oregano, dill, sage and marjoram.

Seeds Useful seeds to keep on hand are caraway, celery and dill.

Spices You will want to stock cinnamon, cumin, ginger, mace, powdered mustard, nutmeg, paprika, curry powder and chili powder.

Peppers There are many kinds and forms of peppers, but the basic ones you need are red pepper flakes, ground white pepper and black peppercorns. Keep some of the peppercorns in a mill and save some to be used whole in stocks or soups.

Room-temperature pantry Yellow onions, russet or white potatoes and garlic are basic items to soupmaking, and they keep at room temperature long enough to deserve a mention here. Store away from excessive warmth or moisture in a dark, well-ventilated place.

Refrigerated pantry Fresh carrots, celery and parsley are repeatedly called for in soup recipes. Keep these on hand in your crisper.

Grains, legumes and pasta Keep an assortment of colorful grains, legumes and pasta in glass jars on your pantry shelf to inspire your soupmaking. I suggest brown rice (plain and basmati), white rice, wheat, barley, black or turtle beans, Great Northern beans, lentils, navy beans, pinto beans, split peas, macaroni, egg noodles (plain and spinach) and tiny alphabet pasta for the kids.

Soup Cookery Seminar

The whys and wherefores of soupmaking techniques

Soupmaking is one of the most forgiving of kitchen technologies. You need not measure with exactitude or cook with precision to produce a bubbling potful of heartwarming soup. With the understanding of a few basic methods, you can be a soupmaker par excellence.

Cutting vegetables for soup   Don't cut vegetables for all soups the same shape or size. Your eye would become quickly bored with your handiwork. Chunks of vegetables will give a soup a rustic character; a dainty cut is more suitable for something elegant. Cut all of the vegetables for any one soup in the same general style to avoid a discordant appearance.

To peel or not to peel carrots   I'm leaving this choice up to you. The reason is that it doesn't matter. If you merely scrub your carrots, they will retain a bit more fiber and vitamins, but if you are used to peeling them for looks, go right ahead; it just doesn't make that much difference.

Precooking vegetables before adding stocks   In most recipes you either will *sauté* the aromatic vegetables in a small amount of fat or will *sweat* the vegetables over low to medium heat, with the lid slightly ajar. Both processes seal in and intensify food flavors. In the case of onions and garlic, sautéing removes some of the strong flavors and replaces them with sweeter, more pleasant ones.

Peeling tomatoes   Pour boiling water over whole tomatoes, rinse them quickly in cool water and peel. A garden-ripe tomato can also be coaxed to part with its skin if you first drag a chef's or paring knife firmly over the skin making sure to cover all parts. Hold the knife blade perpendicular to the skin while you drag it. Then peel.

Seeding tomatoes   Cut a peeled tomato in half. Turn each half upside-down over the sink and squeeze gently, expelling the seeds.

Sautéing mushrooms   Mushrooms will first soak up whatever butter they are cooked in and will appear quite dry. If you continue to cook them while stirring, they release some of their moisture, so that they do not burn, but cook evenly.

Cooking beans for soup   Several of the soups and chilis list the canned bean alternative to home-cooked (from dried) beans. One of the advantages of home-cooking (in addition to saving money) is that you can control the salt that is added for flavor. (Don't add salt or any acids, such as tomato sauce, to dried beans before they are thoroughly cooked, as these ingredients can prevent the beans from becoming tender.) To cook dried beans: Cover the beans with water that is three times the measurement of the beans to be cooked. Soak for 6 to 8 hours, or overnight. Drain the beans. Add the same amount of water as before and slowly bring the beans to a full boil. Reduce the heat to a simmer and cook, covered, for 1 to 3 hours, or until the beans are tender.

If you forget to soak the beans ahead of time, bring them to a boil with the soaking water and boil for 2 minutes. Remove from the heat and let the beans stand for 1 hour. Drain, cover with water, and cook as before. To cut it down even more, boil the beans for 5 minutes, and soak for just 30 minutes before draining.

One pound of dried beans will produce about 6 cups of home-cooked. You can expect to produce 2 cups cooked beans with each ⅔ cup dried you use. Cooked beans can be frozen in 2-cup quantities for later use. Covered tightly after they have cooled, cooked beans will keep in the refrigerator for up to 5 days.

One 14- to 16-ounce can of canned beans can be used for each 2 cups of cooked beans called for. If you wish to remove the sodium from canned beans, rinse and drain them before use. If sodium is not a problem for you, you may prefer to keep the gravy the beans are canned in.

Simmering soups Soups develop their best flavor if they are simmered gently for as long as it takes to cook them. Heavy saucepans and stockpots help prevent too-rapid heating, but it is often difficult to maintain a gentle simmer. Leave the lid slightly ajar to avoid a heat build up, if necessary.

Removing the bay leaf Be sure to remove the bay leaf from your soups before serving. A bay leaf will retain its sharp edges, even when broken into small pieces and should never be left in soup that is served.

Removing fats Fats can be skimmed from hot soups, using a flat spoon or skimmer. If soups are chilled, the fat will solidify on the top, making it easy to remove before reheating. To cut down on fats in general, always use the lighter ingredient when a choice is given.

Thickening soups Soups can be thickened by pureeing the ingredients after cooking. This type of thickened soup may separate as it settles. Additional thickening agents can be employed to keep the puree in suspension; the easiest to use is cornstarch.

Stir cornstarch into cold water or other liquid, using 2 tablespoons of liquid for every 1 tablespoon of cornstarch used. Then stir this slurry into the simmering soup. Continue to cook, stirring, for about 2 minutes, or until the soup is thickened. If you continue to cook and stir a soup already thickened with cornstarch, it may thin again.

Flour and butter, employed together, make an excellent thickener. They can be cooked together with liquid to make a sauce, such as béchamel, or they can be added to a soup at the end of cooking in the form of a kneaded butter-flour mixture called *beurre manié*.

To make a béchamel, stir equal amounts of butter and flour together in a saucepan over low to medium heat. Cook, stirring, for 2 to 5 minutes, or until the mixture is bubbly and just beginning to color a little darker than pasty white. Remove from heat and add *hot* milk, cream or stock, all at once, stirring or whisking constantly while you add the liquid. If the butter and flour mixture is cooked adequately and the liquid is sufficiently hot, the sauce will thicken very quickly. If the flour and butter mixture is cooked until it colors a deep tan before the liquid is added, the thickening power of the flour will be diminished.

To use a *beurre manié,* knead equal amounts of butter and flour together to a smooth paste. While the soup simmers, drop in the mixture, bit by bit, stirring all the while. Cook just until the soup thickens; continued cooking after that point can cause the butter to separate from the flour and float to the top.

Soups will also thicken when their ingredients include any of the following: torn bread, bread crumbs, crushed crackers, pasta, rice, barley, wheat, potatoes, dried beans or lentils.

Melting cheeses   Cheese should be added to soup near the end of the cooking time. Stir cheese gently over low heat just until melted. Brisk stirring can cause a stringy texture and high heat can burn the cheese to the bottom of the pot.

Using lowfat cheeses   I use lowfat cheeses often, but if they don't produce a palatable result, I use full-fat types. That's why you will see lowfat called for in some of the recipes but not in others.

Substitutes for alcoholic flavorings   If you wish to cook without alcohol, substitute a compatible liquid for the eliminated alcohol. If the soup has a chicken or beef stock base, use more of that same stock or water. If the soup already has milk in it, you can use additional milk. If there is only a tablespoonful or two of alcohol used, simply leave it out with no substitute.

Burning the soup   Don't think that you can't burn soup. If the soup is thick and the flame is high, it will burn quickly on the bottom. Soups are more likely to burn while reheating. Always reheat over as gentle a heat as you can and stir frequently. If the soup begins to stick to the bottom of the pot and threatens to burn, transfer it to another pot, leaving the scorched portion behind. With luck, you will leave the burnt flavor with it.

Coming to Terms with Soup

A glossary of words and phrases you may come across in this, and other, soup books

Al dente   Firm to the tooth or bite.

Aromatic vegetables   Onions, garlic, leeks, shallots, carrots and celery, used as the basis of many soups.

Beurre manié   A manipulated or kneaded butter-flour mixture that is added to simmering soups or stews in tiny bits and pieces. Used as a thickening agent at the end of the cooking process.

Bisque   A thin to thick cream soup, made from fish or vegetable purees.

Blend   To stir, rather than beat, ingredients, until they are well combined.

Boil   To cook in a liquid, the surface of which is broken by a continuous bubbling action.

Bouillabaisse   A hearty soup containing several kinds of fish or shellfish, prepared with onions, tomatoes, herbs and spices.

Bouillon   A clear seasoned broth made from poultry, meat, fish or vegetables.

Bouquet garni   A small bundle of fresh herbs tied together with string. Easy to remove from cooked soups if you do not want the appearance of herbs in the broth.

Chili   A thick stew made with meats and/or cooked dried beans, vegetables and grains. Flavored with commercial chili powder or pure ground chiles and other spices.

Chili powder   A blend of spices and herbs, usually including ground chiles, cumin seed, oregano and garlic powder.

Chill   To make cold, not frozen, in the refrigerator.

Chop   To cut into small pieces.

Chowder   A soup, usually containing milk, that contains meat and/or vegetables, with a thickener, such as potatoes or crackers.

Coat   To cover a food lightly, but thoroughly, with either a dry or liquid substance.

Colander   A wide straining device with fewer and larger holes than a sieve.

Combine   To mix or blend two or more ingredients.

Cube   To cut into small, square-sided solids usually from ¼ to ½ inch per side.

Curry powder   A mixture of spices, usually including cumin, coriander, ginger, red or cayenne pepper and turmeric.

Deglaze   To use liquid to loosen food particles and caramelized drippings in the bottom of a pan so that they will be incorporated into a stock, soup or stew.

Dice   To cut into small even cubes, usually no larger than ¼ inch per side.

Dissolve   To make a solution by stirring a solid into a liquid.

Drain   To pour through a strainer or colander and let stand until the liquid is separated from the solids.

Drippings   Fats or other liquids that collect in the bottom of a pan or skillet in a concentrated form.

Garnish   To accompany a dish by decorating attractively with similar or contrasting ingredients.

Gumbo   A thick soup or stew, usually containing okra.

Legumes   Beans, peas or lentils, fresh or dried.

Marinate   To let stand in a seasoned mixture (marinade) to enhance flavor or tenderize.

Mince   To chop into very fine pieces.

Pinch   As much as can be held between the thumb and forefinger. Less than $\frac{1}{16}$ teaspoon.

Poach   To cook food in a liquid that is barely simmering.

Puree   To process in a food processor or blender, or to force through a sieve or food mill, to produce a thick, smooth mixture.

Roux   A cooked mixture of fat and flour, used for thickening.

Sauté   To cook briefly, stirring, in a small amount of hot fat.

Shred   To cut into very thin pieces.

Sieve   A straining device made with fine-mesh wire. Also called strainer.

Simmer   To cook a liquid, not quite at the boiling point. The surface should show only an occasional bubble.

Skim   To remove a substance from the surface of a liquid.

Slurry   A suspension of a solid in a liquid such as cornstarch in water.

Sour salt   Another name for citric acid.

Stews   Thick, savory mixtures, usually using meats as a base, but can be made with vegetables alone.

Stock   The strained liquid in which meat, poultry, fish, bones and/ or vegetables have long-simmered with herbs and seasonings.

Sweat   A term used to denote cooking aromatic vegetables in a small amount of fat and the steam that comes off them in a partially covered pot.

Tureen   A decorative vessel for serving soup.

Vegetable soups   Made with mostly vegetables, but may contain meat, poultry or fish parts or stocks.

Vegetarian soups   Made with vegetables, containing no meat, poultry or fish parts or stocks.

Zest   The outer colored layer of citrus skins. It does not include the white pith found below the colored portion.

The Recipes

Homemade Stocks

For the very best of flavors

Don't feel that you *have* to make stock to make soup—there's always canned broth to fall back on. But, by investing a minimum amount of your own time, you can produce some wonderful beginnings for your soup cookery. Simply let a pot of stock ingredients simmer at the back of the stove on a day when you are doing other things. Even the busiest of cooks can manage that.

Beef Bone Stock

I prefer to buy my meat on the bone and bone it myself, leaving meaty bones for the stockpot. Many markets today receive their meat already boned. In that case, ask your butcher for help or look for packages marked: oxtails, beef ribs or soup bones.

5-quart stockpot
Makes 3 quarts

2 TABLESPOONS EXTRA-VIRGIN OLIVE OIL
4 POUNDS MEATY BEEF BONES
4 QUARTS COLD WATER
1 YELLOW ONION, UNPEELED AND COARSELY CHOPPED
2 CARROTS, COARSELY CHOPPED
2 CELERY RIBS, COARSELY CHOPPED
3 FRESH PARSLEY SPRIGS
2 FRESH THYME SPRIGS, OR ¼ TEASPOON DRIED
1 WHOLE CLOVE
1 BAY LEAF
4 WHOLE BLACK PEPPERCORNS
1 TEASPOON SALT (OPTIONAL)

1. Warm the oil in the stockpot over medium-high heat. Add the beef bones, one layer at a time, and brown on all sides. Remove the bones to a dish as they brown. When the last of the bones are browned, pour the cold water into the pot and stir to loosen any browned bits that may be stuck to the bottom.

2. Return the bones to the pot. Slowly bring to a gentle boil. Skim the surface of the water as foam rises to the top. When the foam subsides, add all of the remaining ingredients. Cook at a simmer, with the lid slightly ajar, for 4 hours.

3. Remove the pot from the heat. Use a slotted spoon or tongs to remove the bones from the pot. Strain the stock and pour into quart-size containers; cool. Cover and refrigerate. The stock will keep in the refrigerator for 3 days. It may be frozen for later use.

Brown Stock

This stock is made with the same ingredients used for beef bone stock, but the browning process yields a deeper flavor. The two stocks may be used interchangeably.

5-quart stockpot
Makes 3 quarts

USE THE INGREDIENTS LISTED UNDER BEEF BONE STOCK (PRECEDING RECIPE).

1. Instead of browning the bones in the stockpot, pour the olive oil in a roasting pan and roll the bones in it. Brown the bones in a 400°F oven for 1 hour, or until evenly browned on all sides.

2. Transfer the browned bones to the stockpot. Use some of the water to help scrape up any browned bits that remain in the roasting pan; add the mixture to the stockpot. Proceed as before.

Cheapskate Chicken Stock

Nothing beats homemade when it comes to chicken stock. The backs and necks used here are most economical. If you feel flush, you can use a larger stockpot and a 6-pound stewing hen instead, doubling the rest of the ingredients used.

5-quart stockpot
Makes 3 quarts

4 POUNDS CHICKEN BACKS AND NECKS
4 QUARTS COLD WATER
1 YELLOW ONION, UNPEELED AND COARSELY CHOPPED
2 CARROTS, COARSELY CHOPPED
2 CELERY RIBS, COARSELY CHOPPED
1 GARLIC CLOVE, COARSELY CHOPPED
1 BAY LEAF
2 WHOLE BLACK PEPPERCORNS
2 FRESH LEMON THYME SPRIGS (THERE IS NO PERFECT HERBAL
    SUBSTITUTE. IF YOU CAN'T GET THIS, USE 1 FRESH THYME SPRIG
    OR ⅛ TEASPOON DRIED AND 1 SLICE OF LEMON.)
4 FRESH PARSLEY SPRIGS
½ TEASPOON SALT (OPTIONAL)

1. Rinse the chicken under cold running water and place in the stockpot. Add the cold water to cover. Slowly bring to a gentle boil. Skim the surface of the water as the foam rises to the top. When the foam subsides, add all of the remaining ingredients. Cook at a simmer, with the lid slightly ajar, for 2 hours.

2. Remove the pot from the heat. Use a slotted spoon or tongs to remove the pieces of chicken. Strain the stock and pour into quart-size containers; cool. Cover and refrigerate. The stock will keep in the refrigerator for up to 3 days. It may be frozen for later use.

Turkey Carcass Stock

Throwing away a turkey carcass without using it to make stock is a waste of a valuable resource. The stock is rich and flavorful, and probably the easiest of all to make. The directions are based on a carcass from a roasted 18-pound bird. Use the same recipe for the remains from 2 ducks or 3 chickens.

5-quart stockpot
Makes 2 to 3 quarts

1 TURKEY CARCASS
2 TO 3 QUARTS COLD WATER
1 CARROT, CHOPPED
2 CELERY RIBS WITH LEAVES, CHOPPED
1 YELLOW ONION, UNPEELED AND COARSELY CHOPPED
½ BAY LEAF
2 FRESH LEMON THYME SPRIGS (THERE IS NO PERFECT HERBAL
   SUBSTITUTE. IF YOU CAN'T GET THIS, USE 1 FRESH THYME SPRIG
   OR ⅛ TEASPOON DRIED AND 1 SLICE LEMON.)
3 PARSLEY SPRIGS
½ TEASPOON SALT (OPTIONAL)

1. Break the turkey carcass into small pieces so that the bones will
fit compactly in the stockpot. Use both bones and skin, but rinse off any
stuffing that may cling to the pieces. Place in the stockpot with all of the
remaining ingredients, using only enough water to cover. Slowly bring to
a boil. Reduce the heat to a simmer and cook, with the lid slightly ajar, for
2 hours. Remove from the heat.

2. Use a slotted spoon or tongs to remove the larger pieces of
carcass from the pot. Strain the stock and pour into quart-size containers;
cool. Cover and refrigerate. The stock will keep in the refrigerator for 3
days. It may be frozen for later use.

Ham Bone Stock

The best part about cooking a whole ham is the reward of a meaty bone
when the ham slices are gone. Use the bone to make this stock and store
it in the freezer. It will be ready when needed for cooking a pot of bean or
split pea soup when time and mood allow.

33

5-quart stockpot
Makes 2 quarts

2 POUNDS MEATY HAM BONES
3 QUARTS COLD WATER
2 MEDIUM ONIONS, UNPEELED AND COARSELY CHOPPED
2 MEDIUM CARROTS, COARSELY CHOPPED
2 CELERY RIBS WITH LEAVES, COARSELY CHOPPED
1 MEDIUM RUSSET OR WHITE POTATO, COARSELY CHOPPED
1 SMALL TURNIP, COARSELY CHOPPED
1 GARLIC CLOVE, CRUSHED
1 BAY LEAF
3 BLACK PEPPERCORNS
4 FRESH PARSLEY SPRIGS
2 FRESH THYME SPRIGS, OR 1/4 TEASPOON DRIED

1. Place the ham bones and cold water in the stockpot. Slowly bring to a gentle boil. Skim the surface of the water as the foam rises to the top. When the foam subsides, add all of the remaining ingredients. Cook at a simmer, with the lid slightly ajar, for 4 hours.

2. Remove from the heat. With a slotted spoon or tongs, remove the ham bones from the pot. Strain the stock and pour into quart-size containers; cool. Cover and refrigerate. The stock will keep in the refrigerator for 3 days. It may be frozen for later use.

Free-Form Stockpot

In order to save money, you may wish to save meat trimmings and bones in a bag in your freezer, waiting until you have a sufficient quantity to make a pot of stock. There is no reason why beef and poultry bones cannot be combined in such a venture. Bones from roasted meats can be mixed with the uncooked. A few pork bones can be included, but if many are used, the stock will be unpleasantly sweet. Ham is too assertive and should be reserved for recipes designed for its use.

5-quart stockpot
Makes 3 quarts

4 POUNDS BONES AND TRIMMINGS FROM BEEF AND POULTRY
4 QUARTS COLD WATER
1 YELLOW ONION, UNPEELED AND COARSELY CHOPPED
1 CARROT, COARSELY CHOPPED
2 CELERY RIBS WITH LEAVES, COARSELY CHOPPED
3 FRESH PARSLEY SPRIGS
2 FRESH THYME OR LEMON THYME SPRIGS, OR ¼ TEASPOON DRIED
1 WHOLE CLOVE
1 BAY LEAF
3 WHOLE BLACK PEPPERCORNS
½ TEASPOON SALT (OPTIONAL)

1. Place the bones and cold water in the stockpot and slowly bring to a gentle boil. Skim the surface of the water as the foam rises to the top. When the foam subsides, add all of the remaining ingredients. Cook at a simmer, with the lid slightly ajar, for 3 hours.

2. Remove the pot from heat. Use a slotted spoon or tongs to remove the bones. Strain the stock and pour into quart-size containers; cool. Cover and refrigerate. The stock will keep in the refrigerator for 3 days. It may be frozen for later use.

Hearty Vegetable Stock

Some cooks prefer to avoid animal products entirely. This is a full-bodied stock that can be used in place of any meat stock. Use a 5-quart stockpot and double the recipe, if desired.

3-quart saucepan
Makes 1 quart

1 TABLESPOON EXTRA-VIRGIN OLIVE OIL
2 CARROTS, COARSELY CHOPPED
2 CELERY RIBS, COARSELY CHOPPED
1 LARGE YELLOW ONION, UNPEELED AND COARSELY CHOPPED
1½ QUARTS COLD WATER
1 MEDIUM TURNIP, COARSELY CHOPPED
1 MEDIUM RUSSET OR WHITE POTATO, PEELED AND COARSELY
   CHOPPED
3 FRESH PARSLEY SPRIGS
1 FRESH THYME SPRIG, OR ⅛ TEASPOON DRIED
¼ TEASPOON SALT (OPTIONAL)

1. Warm the oil in the saucepan over medium heat. Add the carrots, celery and onion and cook, stirring, for 2 to 3 minutes. Reduce the heat to low, partially cover the pan and cook the vegetables for 5 to 10 minutes, until soft.

2. Add all of the remaining ingredients. Bring to a gentle boil. Reduce the heat to a simmer, and cook, with the lid slightly ajar, for 2 to 3 hours.

3. Strain the stock and pour into a quart-size container; cool. Cover and refrigerate. The stock will keep in the refrigerator for 3 days. It may be frozen for later use.

Summer Vegetable Stock

You can vary the ingredients in this stock, if you wish. Asparagus trimmings and mushrooms stems make fine additions. Beware of spinach, cauliflower, cabbage or broccoli, however, as they may overpower the flavor of your stock.

3-quart saucepan
Makes 1 quart

2 CARROTS, COARSELY CHOPPED
2 CELERY RIBS, COARSELY CHOPPED
3 SCALLIONS WITH THE GREEN TOPS, SLICED
2 ZUCCHINI, COARSELY CHOPPED
1 HEAD LOOSE-LEAF LETTUCE, CHOPPED
1 FRESH DILL SPRIG
1 FRESH THYME SPRIG
1 FRESH SUMMER SAVORY SPRIG
1½ QUARTS COLD WATER
¼ TEASPOON SALT (OPTIONAL)

1. Combine all of the ingredients in the saucepan. Bring to a gentle boil. Reduce the heat to a simmer and cook, with the lid slightly ajar, for 2 hours.

2. Strain the stock and pour into a quart-size container; cool. Cover and refrigerate. The stock will keep in the refrigerator for up to 3 days. It may be frozen for later use.

Fish Frame Stock

Fish stock does not keep well. Make it right before you want to use it for the best fresh flavor. Use parts from nonoily, white-fleshed fish, such as perch, halibut, flounder or sole. Shellfish shells are desirable additions when available. Be sure that whatever fish or shellfish parts you use are fresh, not fishy. The gills, the fishiest part of the fish, should be removed before the heads are added to the pot.

3-quart nonreactive saucepan
Makes 1 quart

1 CUP DRY WHITE WINE
4 CUPS COLD WATER
2 POUNDS FISH HEADS (GILLS REMOVED) AND FISH FRAMES OR
   SKELETONS
1 YELLOW ONION, THINLY SLICED
1 CARROT, THINLY SLICED
1 CELERY RIB, THINLY SLICED
1 LEMON, SEEDED AND THINLY SLICED
4 FRESH PARSLEY SPRIGS
¼ TEASPOON SALT (OPTIONAL)

1. Combine the wine, cold water and fish in the saucepan. Slowly bring to a gentle boil. Skim off any foam that rises. When the foam subsides, add all of the remaining ingredients. Lower the heat to a simmer, and cook, with the lid slightly ajar, for 30 minutes.

2. Strain the stock and pour into a quart-size container; cool. Cover and refrigerate. The stock will keep in the refrigerator for 1 to 2 days. It does not freeze well.

Clam Juice Stock

Bottled clam juice comes to the rescue for the cook who wants to make fish stock and who lives in a part of the country where fish trimmings are hard to come by. If you're in a hurry, combine the first three ingredients and use without cooking.

3-quart nonreactive saucepan
Makes 1 quart

3 CUPS BOTTLED CLAM JUICE

1 CUP COLD WATER

½ CUP DRY WHITE WINE

1 YELLOW ONION, COARSELY CHOPPED

1 CARROT, COARSELY CHOPPED

1 CELERY RIB, COARSELY CHOPPED

1 BLACK PEPPERCORN

1. Combine all of the ingredients in the saucepan. Simmer, with the lid slightly ajar, for 45 to 60 minutes.

2. Strain the stock and pour into a quart-size container. This is best used soon after it is made.

Satisfying Vegetable Soups

For all occasions

Vegetable soups can be very palate satisfying and are a wonderful means of cutting down on meat in our diets. I find it interesting that diners who turn up their nose at something called a vegetable plate often relish a vegetable soup. Do you think it's sneaky not to point out that they are basically the same?

There is a difference between a vegetable soup and a vegetarian soup. All vegetable soups are not vegetarian. Many use meat-based stocks and some use bacon or soup bones for flavor. If desired, the meat-based stocks in this chapter can be replaced with vegetable stock or plain water and the animal fats that are used can be replaced with a vegetable oil.

Tomato Bouillon

Breakfast doesn't have to be bacon and eggs or boring, high-fiber cereal. For a welcome change, drink a mug of hot tomato bouillon. Serve with biscuits, muffins or scones.

5-quart nonreactive stockpot
Makes 1 quart/3 moderate servings

12 RED–RIPE TOMATOES, QUARTERED

½ CUP COLD WATER

1 SMALL YELLOW ONION, CHOPPED

1 CELERY RIB, CHOPPED

3 FRESH PARSLEY SPRIGS

3 FRESH BASIL SPRIGS

½ BAY LEAF

SALT AND PEPPER, TO TASTE

FRESH BASIL SPRIGS, FOR GARNISH

1. Combine the tomatoes, water, onion, celery, parsley, basil and bay leaf in the stockpot. Bring to a gentle boil, stirring occasionally to prevent sticking. When the juices start to flow, reduce the heat to a simmer and cook, with the lid slightly ajar, for about 30 minutes, or until the tomatoes are completely cooked. The long cooking makes the pulp easier to strain.

2. Run the mixture through a food mill or press through a sieve with the back of a wooden spoon. Taste and add salt and pepper, if desired. Serve hot in heavy mugs or double-handled soup cups, so diners can drink the soup if they wish. Insert a sprig of fresh basil for garnish.

Chunky Gazpacho

This soup is usually served as a first course, in lieu of a salad. After one of our sultry August days, I like it as a light supper with whole-grain bread-and-butter sandwiches.

no-cook
Makes 1½ quarts/6 appetizer or 4 moderate servings

1 CAN (8 OUNCES) TOMATO SAUCE

2 CUPS HOMEMADE BEEF STOCK OR CANNED BROTH

2 TABLESPOONS FRESH LEMON JUICE

2 TABLESPOONS EXTRA-VIRGIN OLIVE OIL

1 TEASPOON WORCESTERSHIRE SAUCE

DASH OF HOT PEPPER SAUCE, OR TO TASTE

3 LARGE TOMATOES, PEELED, SEEDED AND DICED

1 GREEN BELL PEPPER, SEEDED AND DICED

1 CUCUMBER, DICED (SKIN LEFT ON IF HOMEGROWN)

2 SCALLIONS, THINLY SLICED

CHOPPED CHIVES, FOR GARNISH

1. In a nonreactive 2-quart bowl, stir together the tomato sauce, stock, lemon juice, olive oil, Worcestershire, and hot pepper sauce. Add the tomatoes, bell pepper, cucumber and scallions and stir again. Refrigerate to chill.

2. Serve in small bowls nestled in larger bowls that have been filled with cracked ice. Pass the chives.

Tomato and Bread Soup with Pesto

I recently enjoyed lunch at Cafe Spiaggia in Chicago where my companions and I tasted a delightful soup called Pomodori e Pane (Tomato and Bread). I have duplicated it for you here. The flavor reminds me of old-fashioned stewed tomatoes.

3-quart nonreactive saucepan
Makes 5 cups/4 moderate servings

1 TEASPOON EXTRA-VIRGIN OLIVE OIL

3 TABLESPOONS FINELY CHOPPED ONION

6 LARGE TOMATOES, PEELED, SEEDED AND CHOPPED

2 CUPS HOMEMADE CHICKEN STOCK OR CANNED BROTH

2 TEASPOONS SUGAR

1 SLICE FRESH WHOLE WHEAT BREAD, TORN INTO SMALL PIECES

SALT AND PEPPER, TO TASTE

PESTO (RECIPE FOLLOWS)

1. Heat the oil, add the onion and cook in the saucepan over medium-high heat, stirring often, until tender, about 2 minutes. Add the tomatoes, stock, sugar and torn bread. Simmer, covered, until the tomatoes are cooked, 7 to 10 minutes.

2. Taste and add salt and pepper, if desired. Swirl a spoonful of pesto into each serving.

Pesto

You will need a food processor to make this recipe. I like to make jar after jar when the basil is growing bushy in midsummer and pack it into small freezer-safe jelly jars. Whenever I need pesto I retrieve one of the jars, use what I need and return the unused portion to the freezer.

no-cook
Makes 1 cup

2 GARLIC CLOVES, PEELED

2 CUPS FIRMLY PACKED WASHED AND DRIED FRESH BASIL LEAVES

2 TABLESPOONS DRY-ROASTED SUNFLOWER SEEDS (OPTIONAL)

½ CUP FRESHLY GRATED PARMESAN CHEESE

ABOUT ½ CUP EXTRA-VIRGIN OLIVE OIL

1. With the machine running, drop the garlic cloves through the feed tube of a food processor to chop. Stop the machine, add the basil and the sunflower seeds and process until finely chopped. Add the Parmesan and

pulse to mix. With the machine running, add just enough of the oil through the feed tube to make the pesto smooth and creamy.

2. Transfer the pesto to a glass jar. Run a knife down the edges of the jar to eliminate any air pockets. Smooth the top of the pesto and cover with a thin film of olive oil to prevent oxidation. Cover tightly and store in the refrigerator for up to 1 week or in the freezer for up to 6 months.

Green Tomato Soup

Green tomatoes make a tasty early summer soup while you're waiting for the fruit to turn red.

3-quart nonreactive saucepan
Makes 1 quart/4 appetizer servings

2 TEASPOONS EXTRA-VIRGIN OLIVE OIL
1 YELLOW ONION, CHOPPED
1 CARROT, DICED
2 CUPS HOMEMADE CHICKEN STOCK OR CANNED BROTH
1 CAN (8 OUNCES) TOMATO SAUCE
2 CUPS DICED GREEN TOMATOES (ABOUT 1 POUND BEFORE DICING)
1 TEASPOON CHOPPED FRESH DILL, OR $1/4$ TEASPOON DRIED
1 TEASPOON FRESH LEMON JUICE
1 TEASPOON SUGAR
SALT AND PEPPER, TO TASTE
THIN LEMON SLICES, FOR GARNISH

1. Heat the oil in the saucepan over medium heat. Add the onion and the carrot and sauté, with the lid slightly ajar, until the onion is tender, 5 to 7 minutes.

2. Stir in the stock, tomato sauce, tomatoes, dill, lemon juice and sugar. Cover and simmer for 15 minutes, or just until the tomatoes are tender.

3. Add salt and pepper to taste. Serve in small soup cups. Float a slice of lemon on each serving.

Garden Plot Soup

This soup allows you to use whatever is fresh and good from the garden or market. Onions, celery, carrots and tomatoes should be included every time you make the soup. The remaining vegetables called for may be substituted at will—fresh garden peas, when available, are delightful. Whole wheat bread and some fresh fruit is all that you need to finish the meal.

5-quart stockpot
Makes 3 quarts/8 moderate servings

2 TABLESPOONS EXTRA-VIRGIN OLIVE OIL

4 GARLIC CLOVES, MINCED

2 YELLOW ONIONS, CHOPPED

2 QUARTS HOMEMADE CHICKEN OR VEGETABLE STOCK, CANNED BROTH OR WATER

3 CELERY RIBS, CHOPPED

3 CARROTS, CHOPPED

3 RED-RIPE TOMATOES, PEELED, SEEDED AND CHOPPED

1 CUP CHOPPED BROCCOLI STEMS AND FLORETS

1 CUP CHOPPED GREEN BEANS

1/4 CUP CHOPPED FRESH BASIL (DO NOT USE DRIED)

1/4 CUP CHOPPED FRESH PARSLEY

1 TABLESPOON CHOPPED FRESH SUMMER SAVORY (THERE IS NO SUBSTITUTE FOR THIS, BUT THE SOUP CAN BE MADE WITHOUT IT.)

1/2 TEASPOON DILL SEEDS

4 OUNCES EGG NOODLES OR SPINACH NOODLES

1 CUP SLICED ZUCCHINI

SALT AND PEPPER, TO TASTE

1. Heat the oil in the stockpot over medium-high heat. Add the garlic and onions and cook, stirring, until the onions are tender, 3 to 4 minutes. Add the stock, celery, carrots, tomatoes, broccoli, green beans, basil, parsley, savory and dill seeds and bring to a simmer. Cover and cook until the vegetables are just crisp-tender, about 10 minutes.

2. Add the noodles and cook, stirring occasionally, until al dente, about 7 minutes. Add the zucchini and cook until just crisp-tender, about 2 minutes. Add salt and pepper to taste. Serve in heavy pottery bowls.

Winter Vegetable Soup

This soup is filled to the brim with chunky vegetables—just right for a cold winter day.

3-quart saucepan
Makes 2 quarts/6 moderate servings

1 TABLESPOON EXTRA-VIRGIN OLIVE OIL

1 YELLOW ONION, COARSELY CHOPPED

1 QUART HOMEMADE BEEF STOCK OR CANNED BROTH

2 CARROTS, CUT DIAGONALLY INTO ½-INCH SLICES

2 CELERY RIBS, CUT DIAGONALLY INTO ½-INCH SLICES

2 MEDIUM RUSSET OR WHITE POTATOES, PEELED AND CUT INTO CHUNKS

2 TOMATOES, PEELED, SEEDED AND CHOPPED

2 CUPS COARSELY CHOPPED CABBAGE

½ TEASPOON CHOPPED FRESH THYME, OR ¼ TEASPOON DRIED

1 BAY LEAF

1 TEASPOON RED WINE VINEGAR

1 TEASPOON SUGAR

SALT AND PEPPER, TO TASTE

1. Heat the oil in the saucepan over medium heat. Add the onion and cook, stirring now and then, until tender, 5 to 7 minutes.

2. Stir in the stock, carrots, celery, potatoes, tomatoes, cabbage, thyme, bay leaf, vinegar and sugar. Simmer, covered, for 20 minutes, or until the vegetables are tender.

3. Remove the bay leaf. Add salt and pepper to taste. Serve in flat soup plates.

Cool-as-a-Cucumber Soup

This soup is wonderfully refreshing on a hot summer day—no cooking and very few calories. If you grow your own cucumbers, you can leave them unpeeled. My garden-grown burpless cucumbers are delicious, peels and all.

no-cook
Makes 5 cups/4 moderate servings

3 MEDIUM CUCUMBERS (ABOUT 1½ POUNDS)
2 CUPS PLAIN LOWFAT YOGURT
2 CUPS HOMEMADE CHICKEN STOCK OR CANNED BROTH
1 TABLESPOON FRESH LEMON JUICE
1 TABLESPOON FINELY CHOPPED FRESH CHIVES
1 TEASPOON MINCED FRESH DILL, OR ½ TEASPOON DRIED
SALT AND PEPPER, TO TASTE

1. Peel, seed and dice the cucumbers; you will have about 3 cups. Put them into a sieve to drain.

2. In a 1½-quart nonreactive bowl or container, stir the yogurt until smooth. Gradually stir in the stock. Add the cucumbers, lemon juice, chives and dill. Cover and refrigerate until well chilled, several hours or overnight.

3. When ready to serve, stir gently and add salt and pepper, if desired. Serve in chilled soup cups.

Country Cabbage Soup

This is simple peasant fare. Serve with crusty bread, fruit and cheese.

3-quart nonreactive saucepan
Makes 2 quarts/6 moderate servings

1 TABLESPOON EXTRA-VIRGIN OLIVE OIL
2 YELLOW ONIONS, CHOPPED
1 QUART HOMEMADE CHICKEN STOCK OR CANNED BROTH
8 CUPS COARSELY SHREDDED FRESH YOUNG CABBAGE (ABOUT 1 POUND)*
1 CAN (8 OUNCES) TOMATO SAUCE
1/2 TEASPOON CARAWAY SEEDS
1/2 TEASPOON DILL SEEDS
SALT AND PEPPER, TO TASTE

1. Heat the oil in the saucepan. Add the onions and sauté, with the lid slightly ajar, until the onions are tender, 5 to 7 minutes.
2. Stir in the stock, cabbage, tomato sauce, caraway seeds and dill seeds. Simmer, covered, for 20 minutes, or until the cabbage is tender.
3. Add salt and pepper, to taste. Serve in flat soup plates.

Sauerkraut Soup

Sauerkraut can be overpowering in a soup. Rinsing it in hot water before use gives it a clean, fresh taste. Serve with bratwurst on a bun for "soup and a sandwich."

*Be sure the cabbage is fresh and young. Old cabbage will give the soup an unpleasantly strong flavor.

3-quart nonreactive saucepan
Makes 1½ quarts/4 moderate servings

1 TABLESPOON EXTRA-VIRGIN OLIVE OIL
1 YELLOW ONION, CHOPPED
2 CARROTS, SLICED
1 QUART HOMEMADE CHICKEN STOCK OR CANNED BROTH
1 CAN (12 OUNCES) BEER
2 CUPS FRESH SAUERKRAUT (1 POUND), RINSED IN HOT WATER
   AND DRAINED
2 MEDIUM RUSSET OR WHITE POTATOES, PEELED AND CUBED
1 TABLESPOON CHOPPED FRESH PARSLEY
SALT AND PEPPER, TO TASTE

1. Heat the oil in the saucepan over medium heat. Add the onion and carrots and sauté, with the lid slightly ajar, until the onion is tender, 5 to 7 minutes.

2. Stir in the stock, beer, sauerkraut, potatoes and parsley. Simmer, covered, for 20 to 30 minutes, or until the potatoes are tender.

3. Add salt and pepper, to taste. Serve in heavy pottery bowls.

Peasant Potato Soup

Unpeeled potatoes give this soup a nut-like flavor, enhanced by a sprinkling of chopped walnuts. This is good with sour rye bread and butter. Offer apricot jam.

3-quart saucepan
Makes 1½ quarts/4 moderate servings

2 TABLESPOONS EXTRA-VIRGIN OLIVE OIL
1 YELLOW ONION, FINELY CHOPPED
4 LARGE RUSSET OR WHITE POTATOES, WELL-SCRUBBED
1 QUART HOMEMADE BEEF STOCK OR CANNED BROTH, HEATED
   UNTIL HOT
SALT AND PEPPER, TO TASTE
4 TABLESPOONS CHOPPED WALNUTS, FOR GARNISH

1. Warm the oil in the saucepan over medium-high heat. Add the onion and cook, stirring constantly, until tender, 4 to 6 minutes. Grate the potatoes into the pan and stir until evenly mixed with the onions.

2. Stir in the stock. Cover and simmer until the potatoes are fork-tender, about 30 minutes.

3. Season to taste with salt and pepper. Spoon into flat soup plates and garnish each serving with 1 tablespoon of the chopped walnuts.

Polenta Potato Soup

I call this an aerobic inspiration—the idea came to me on one of my long walks. It's simply wonderful with crusty Italian bread.

3-quart saucepan
Makes 5 cups/4 moderate servings

1 QUART HOMEMADE CHICKEN STOCK OR CANNED BROTH
3 MEDIUM RUSSET OR WHITE POTATOES, PEELED AND CUBED
1 SMALL YELLOW ONION, CHOPPED
1 CARROT, CHOPPED
1 CELERY RIB, SLICED
1 GARLIC CLOVE, MINCED

1 TABLESPOON CHOPPED ITALIAN FLAT-LEAF PARSLEY
¼ CUP PLUS 1 TABLESPOON POLENTA OR STONE-GROUND YELLOW
   CORNMEAL
2 TABLESPOONS UNSALTED BUTTER
SALT AND PEPPER, TO TASTE

1. Combine the stock, potatoes, onion, carrot, celery, garlic and parsley in the saucepan. Simmer, covered, until the vegetables are tender, about 30 minutes.

2. Uncover the pot. Sprinkle in the polenta, stirring constantly. Raise the heat so that the mixture bubbles and continue to cook, stirring, until the soup thickens, 3 to 5 minutes. Add the butter and stir to melt. Taste and add salt and pepper, if needed.

New Potato Soup

My garden is not large, but I always plan enough room for a small plot of red or new potatoes. I plant early, with the first lettuce. We start digging them for boiling as soon as any can be found on the roots of the plants. When the tops begin to dry, we dig them all. Some are always smaller than others. I use the smallest ones—about 1 inch in diameter—in this soup.

5-quart stockpot
Makes 2 quarts/6 moderate servings

3 SLICES LEAN BACON, DICED
1 YELLOW ONION, COARSELY CHOPPED
1½ POUNDS SMALL NEW POTATOES, SCRUBBED AND COARSELY
   CHOPPED
8 OUNCES GREEN BEANS, PREFERABLY ROMA, COARSELY CHOPPED
1½ QUARTS HOMEMADE CHICKEN STOCK OR CANNED BROTH
1 TEASPOON CHOPPED FRESH THYME, OR ¼ TEASPOON DRIED
1 TEASPOON CHOPPED FRESH SUMMER SAVORY (THERE IS NO DRIED
   SUBSTITUTE FOR THIS, BUT THE SOUP CAN BE MADE WITHOUT
   IT.)
1 TABLESPOON CHOPPED FRESH PARSLEY
SALT AND PEPPER, TO TASTE

1. In the stockpot, sauté the bacon over medium heat until crisp. Spoon off most of the rendered bacon fat, leaving about 1 tablespoon in the pot with the bacon.

2. Add the onion and cook, stirring, until tender, 5 to 7 minutes. Add the potatoes and cook, stirring continuously, until the potatoes appear to be coated with a little of the fat. Stir in the green beans and then add the stock and herbs.

3. Raise the heat and bring the mixture to a boil. Reduce the heat to a simmer, cover and cook at a low simmer until the potatoes are tender and the soup mellows, 45 to 60 minutes.

4. When ready to serve, add salt and pepper to taste. Serve in flat soup plates.

Vidalia Onion Soup Gratinée

This is lighter than the usual onion soup. It combines mild Vidalia onions with the gentle flavor of light olive oil and chicken stock. Serve, of course, with a chilled glass of the same wine used in the cooking.

3-quart saucepan
Makes 2 quarts/6 moderate servings

3 LARGE (4-INCH DIAMETER) VIDALIA ONIONS
2 TABLESPOONS UNSALTED BUTTER PLUS ADDITIONAL BUTTER FOR
  THE BREAD
2 TABLESPOONS EXTRA-LIGHT OLIVE OIL
1 QUART HOMEMADE CHICKEN STOCK OR CANNED BROTH, HEATED
  UNTIL HOT
¼ CUP DRY WHITE WINE
6 SLICES FRENCH BREAD
SALT AND PEPPER, TO TASTE
6 SLICES LOWFAT SWISS CHEESE

1. Peel the onions, slice very thinly and separate into rings. Heat the butter and the oil in the saucepan. Add the onions and cook, stirring, until wilted, but not browned. They will almost fill the pot at the beginning of cooking, but will cook down to about one-third of their original volume.

2. Add the hot stock and wine. Cover and simmer for 30 to 45 minutes.

3. While the soup is cooking, preheat the oven to 400°F. Spread each slice of bread with butter; toast in the oven until just beginning to brown. Leave the oven on.

4. Taste the soup and add salt and pepper, if needed. Ladle the soup into ovenproof bowls. Float a piece of the toast on each serving. Lay 1 slice of the cheese on each slice of bread. Set the bowls on a baking sheet and place in the hot oven until the cheese melts. Serve at once.

Okra Soup

I like to make this any time I have a little extra okra in my garden. It's wonderful with corn bread.

3-quart saucepan
Makes 1½ quarts/4 moderate servings

3 SLICES LEAN BACON, DICED
2 CUPS THINLY SLICED OKRA (ABOUT 12 OUNCES BEFORE SLICING)
¼ GREEN BELL PEPPER, SEEDED AND DICED
2 CELERY RIBS, DICED
1 QUART HOMEMADE CHICKEN STOCK OR CANNED BROTH, HEATED UNTIL HOT
1 LARGE RED-RIPE TOMATO, PEELED, SEEDED AND CHOPPED
2 TABLESPOONS CHOPPED FRESH PARSLEY
½ BAY LEAF
DASH OF HOT PEPPER SAUCE
SALT AND PEPPER, TO TASTE

1. In the saucepan, cook the bacon over medium heat until crisp. Remove with a slotted spoon and reserve. Spoon out all but 2 tablespoons of the rendered fat. Add the okra, bell pepper and celery and cook, stirring often, until tender, about 7 minutes.

2. Return the bacon to the pot. Add the stock, tomato, parsley, bay leaf and hot pepper sauce. Simmer, covered, for 30 minutes.

3. Add salt and pepper, to taste. Serve in flat soup plates.

Garden Lettuce Soup

My intention is the same every spring. I tell myself that I will thin my lettuce patch as soon as the plants are an inch high, leaving but one plant for every foot of space, so the mature heads will be handsomely full. As the garden grows, my resolve weakens. Why not leave the rows crowded, I reason, to provide thinnings for table use. Before long the lettuce is 12 inches high, not one, and the rows are still crowded. I give much of the excess away, we have daily salads, and, of course, this delightful lettuce soup. It's perfect with chicken salad sandwiches on thin-sliced whole wheat bread.

3-quart saucepan
Makes 5 cups/4 moderate servings

1 QUART HOMEMADE CHICKEN STOCK OR CANNED BROTH
2½ CUPS SHREDDED GARDEN LETTUCE
3 SCALLIONS, SLICED
1 CARROT, DICED
1 CUP FRESH OR FROZEN GREEN PEAS
2 TABLESPOONS ALL-PURPOSE FLOUR
2 TABLESPOONS UNSALTED BUTTER
SALT AND PEPPER, TO TASTE

1. Combine the stock, lettuce, scallions, carrot and the peas in the saucepan. Bring to a simmer, cover and cook for 20 to 30 minutes, or until the vegetables are tender.

2. Knead the flour and the butter together. Uncover the pot and bring the soup to a gentle boil. Drop in small pieces of the *beurre manié* and cook, stirring, until thickened.

3. Add salt and pepper to taste. This is pretty when served in clear glass bowls.

Squash Blossom Soup

Can't wait for your zucchini? Make a pot of soup with the flowers. When harvesting zucchini blossoms, select mostly male flowers. They are the first to appear on the plants. The female flowers, which follow, can be detected by the small lump, or squash baby, just behind them on the stem. Female flowers are also edible, but be sure to leave enough to bear fruit.

3-quart saucepan
Makes 1 quart/4 appetizer servings

1 TABLESPOON EXTRA–VIRGIN OLIVE OIL
1 YELLOW ONION, CHOPPED
3 CUPS COARSELY CHOPPED TRIMMED SQUASH BLOSSOMS (SEE
   INTRODUCTION TO RECIPE)
1 TEASPOON FINELY CHOPPED FRESH ROSEMARY (DO NOT USE
   DRIED)
1 QUART HOMEMADE CHICKEN STOCK OR CANNED BROTH, HEATED
   UNTIL HOT
SALT AND PEPPER, TO TASTE

1. Heat the oil in the saucepan over medium heat. Add the onion and cook, stirring often, until tender, 5 to 7 minutes. Add the blossoms and rosemary and cook, stirring constantly, until the blossoms are limp, 2 to 3 minutes.

2. Stir in the hot stock. Cover and simmer for 5 minutes longer. Taste and add salt and pepper if needed. Serve in small soup cups.

Hearty Soups

With meats, pasta, grains or legumes

These soups have more body than an all-vegetable soup, yet they are not quite as heavy as a stew. Perfect for lunches or for main-course meals in a lighter diet.

Curried Quinoa-Tomato Soup

Quinoa (available in health-food stores and some supermarkets) is an ancient grain that is finding new favor. It is very high in protein, making it a good choice for dieters trying to cut down on meats. In this soup the tiny quinoa seeds simmer into translucent beads that resemble miniature bits of pasta. The broth has a just-right tomato flavor that complements the curry seasoning.

Quinoa seeds have a natural covering of saponin that can leave a bitter flavor. Some are prerinsed and some are not. To tell if your seeds retain the saponin, stir a few in a glass of water. If suds occur, the seeds need to be rinsed in several changes of water before use.

3-quart nonreactive saucepan
Makes 2 quarts/6 moderate servings

1 TABLESPOON EXTRA-VIRGIN OLIVE OIL
2 GARLIC CLOVES, MINCED
1 YELLOW ONION, FINELY CHOPPED
1 CELERY RIB, FINELY CHOPPED
2 CUPS FRESH OR CANNED CHOPPED TOMATOES
1½ QUARTS HOMEMADE CHICKEN STOCK OR CANNED BROTH
½ CUP QUINOA SEEDS, RINSED IF NEEDED (SEE ABOVE)
2 TABLESPOONS CORNSTARCH
1½ TEASPOONS CURRY POWDER
¼ CUP COLD WATER
SALT AND PEPPER, TO TASTE
GOLDEN RAISINS, FOR GARNISH

1. Heat the oil in the saucepan over medium heat. Add the garlic, onion and celery, and cook, stirring often, until the onion is tender, 5 to 7 minutes.

2. Stir in the tomatoes, stock and quinoa seeds. Bring to a simmer, cover and cook for 30 minutes.

3. Combine the cornstarch and curry powder. Stir in the cold water. Stir this slurry into the soup and bring to a boil, stirring. Stir for about 2 minutes, or until thickened.

4. Add salt and pepper to taste. Serve in flat bowls, garnished with a sprinkling of golden raisins.

Vegetable Barley Soup

The naturally nutty flavor of barley is enhanced by sautéing it with the aromatic vegetables at the start of this soup.

3-quart saucepan
Makes 1½ quarts/4 moderate servings

1 TABLESPOON UNSALTED BUTTER
2 TABLESPOONS EXTRA-VIRGIN OLIVE OIL
½ CUP BARLEY
1 YELLOW ONION, CHOPPED
2 CARROTS, DICED
2 CELERY RIBS, DICED
1 QUART HOMEMADE CHICKEN STOCK OR CANNED BROTH
SALT AND PEPPER, TO TASTE

1. In the saucepan, melt the butter in the oil over medium heat. Add the barley, onion, carrots and celery and cook, stirring often, until the onion is tender, 7 to 10 minutes.

2. Stir in the stock and bring to a simmer. Cover and cook for 1 to 1½ hours, or until the barley is tender. Add salt and pepper to taste. Serve in rustic pottery bowls.

Turkey Noodle Soup with Old-Fashioned Egg Noodles

The simplicity of this soup lets the flavors of the few homemade ingredients come together in a delicious and satisfying way. If you substitute store-bought stock or noodles, it won't be as successful. Make your own. You'll be glad you did.

5-quart stockpot
Makes 2½ quarts/8 moderate servings

2 QUARTS TURKEY CARCASS STOCK (PAGE 32)
1 BATCH OLD-FASHIONED EGG NOODLES (RECIPE FOLLOWS)
2 TO 3 CUPS DICED COOKED TURKEY MEAT
SALT AND PEPPER, TO TASTE
CHOPPED PARSLEY, FOR GARNISH (OPTIONAL)

1. Bring the stock to a boil. Add the noodles and cook until al dente, about 7 minutes. Add the turkey and cook until heated through.

2. Taste and add salt and pepper, if desired. Serve in heavy pottery bowls. Garnish with parsley, if desired.

Old-Fashioned Egg Noodles

This is a small-batch kind of recipe that is intended to be made and used right away. There's no need to worry about drying the noodles sufficiently to keep on the shelf.

Makes 2 to 4 servings

⅔ CUP UNBLEACHED ALL-PURPOSE FLOUR
PINCH OF SALT (OPTIONAL)
1 LARGE EGG
¼ TEASPOON EXTRA-VIRGIN OLIVE OIL

1. Mix the flour and salt together and mound in a heap. Make a well in the center of the flour mixture and add the egg and oil. Using a fork, stir the egg, gradually bringing in some of the flour until all of the flour is incorporated. You may need to knead it with your hands to capture the last of the flour.

2. Knead the ball of dough on a lightly floured surface until smooth. Dust the dough lightly with flour and enclose in plastic wrap. Set aside to relax for 30 to 45 minutes.

3. On a lightly floured surface, roll out the dough into a 12-inch circle. Cut the circle in half. Cut across the halves to make noodles ¼-inch wide. Let the noodles air-dry for about 30 minutes. Cook as directed in the recipe.

FOOD PROCESSOR TIP: Place the flour and salt in the food processor bowl. Mix the egg and oil together in a measuring cup and pour over the flour mixture. Process until a ball of dough forms on the metal blade. Proceed as before.

Alphabet Soup

Remember how we loved alphabet soup when we were kids. Make a pot of homemade and enjoy it even more. Serve with a basket of assorted crackers.

3-quart nonreactive saucepan
Makes 1¾ quarts/4 moderate servings

1 TABLESPOON EXTRA-VIRGIN OLIVE OIL
1 YELLOW ONION, FINELY CHOPPED
1 GARLIC CLOVE, MINCED
1 QUART HOMEMADE CHICKEN STOCK OR CANNED BROTH
3 CARROTS, SLICED
2 RED-RIPE TOMATOES, PEELED, SEEDED AND CHOPPED
2 TABLESPOONS CHOPPED FRESH PARSLEY
½ CUP ALPHABET MACARONI
1 SMALL ZUCCHINI, CHOPPED
SALT AND PEPPER, TO TASTE
PESTO, TO PASS AT THE TABLE (PAGE 43; OPTIONAL)

1. Heat the oil in the saucepan over medium heat. Add the onion and garlic and cook, stirring often, until the onion is tender, 5 to 7 minutes.

2. Add the stock, carrots, tomatoes and parsley. Bring to a simmer. Cover and cook for 15 minutes.

3. Stir in the macaroni and zucchini and simmer, partially covered, stirring often, for 10 minutes.

4. Add salt and pepper to taste. Serve in white bowls, if available. Pass the pesto at the table for diners to add, if they wish.

Mulligatawny with Raisin-Rice Pilaf

Mulligatawny is a classic East Indian soup. The name means "pepper water." The flavoring is complex. The results are wonderful.

5-quart stockpot
Makes 2 1/2 quarts/6 moderate servings

2 TABLESPOONS EXTRA-VIRGIN OLIVE OIL

2 YELLOW ONIONS, CHOPPED

1 TABLESPOON CURRY POWDER

1 1/2 POUNDS BONELESS, SKINLESS CHICKEN BREASTS, CUT INTO
   BITE-SIZE PIECES

2 QUARTS HOMEMADE CHICKEN STOCK OR CANNED BROTH

3 CARROTS, DICED

2 CELERY RIBS, DICED

2 TABLESPOONS CHOPPED FRESH PARSLEY

1/4 CUP LENTILS, RINSED AND DRAINED

1 GRANNY SMITH APPLE, PEELED, CORED AND DICED

1 TABLESPOON FRESH LEMON JUICE

1 BAY LEAF

1 TEASPOON SUGAR

1/4 TEASPOON GROUND MACE

1/8 TEASPOON GROUND CLOVES

PINCH OF CAYENNE PEPPER

2 TABLESPOONS CORNSTARCH

¼ CUP APPLE JUICE

RAISIN–RICE PILAF, FOR SERVING (RECIPE FOLLOWS)

STORE–BOUGHT FRUIT CHUTNEY, TO PASS AT THE TABLE

1. Heat the oil in the stockpot over medium heat. Add the onions and cook, stirring often, until tender, 5 to 7 minutes.

2. Stir in the curry powder. Add the chicken and stir to coat the pieces with the curry mixture. Add the stock, carrots, celery, parsley, lentils, apple, lemon juice and bay leaf. Bring to a boil. Reduce the heat to a simmer, cover and cook for 45 minutes, or until the lentils are tender.

3. Remove the bay leaf. Stir together the sugar, mace, cloves, cayenne and cornstarch. Stir in the apple juice. Stir the cornstarch mixture into the soup and cook, stirring constantly, until thickened.

4. Serve in flat soup plates. A spoonful of the pilaf can be placed in the bowl before the soup is added, or it can be served as a side dish. Pass the chutney.

Raisin-Rice Pilaf

3-quart saucepan
Makes 3½ cups/6 moderate servings

1 CUP LONG–GRAIN RICE

½ TEASPOON SALT (OPTIONAL)

½ CUP RAISINS

¼ CUP SLIVERED ALMONDS

¼ CUP CHOPPED FRESH PARSLEY

⅛ TEASPOON GROUND CINNAMON

PINCH OF GROUND MACE

1. Combine the rice, salt and 2 cups of water in the saucepan. Bring to a boil. Reduce the heat to a low simmer and cook, covered, for 30 minutes, or until almost all of the water is absorbed by the rice.

2. Remove from the heat. Stir in all of the remaining ingredients with a fork. Cover and let stand for 5 to 10 minutes before serving.

Spaghetti Sauce Soup

When my garden is producing in abundance, I like to start a spaghetti sauce from scratch, simmering slowly until the mixture thickens. When the garden is gone, I simply brown a pound of lean ground beef and stir in a quart of the prepared sauce. It doesn't matter if your sauce is homemade or store-bought, with meat or without; it can combine with aromatic vegetables, herbs, stock and pasta to make this delicious supper soup.

3-quart nonreactive saucepan
Makes 2 quarts/6 moderate servings

2 TABLESPOONS EXTRA-VIRGIN OLIVE OIL
1 YELLOW ONION, CHOPPED
1 GARLIC CLOVE, MINCED
2 CARROTS, CHOPPED
2 CELERY RIBS, CHOPPED
1 TABLESPOON CHOPPED ITALIAN FLAT-LEAF PARSLEY
1 TABLESPOON CHOPPED FRESH BASIL (DRIED IS NO SUBSTITUTE; IF FRESH ISN'T AVAILABLE, LEAVE IT OUT.)
2 CUPS SPAGHETTI SAUCE
1 QUART HOMEMADE CHICKEN STOCK OR CANNED BROTH
4 OUNCES ROTINI PASTA
SALT AND PEPPER, TO TASTE
FRESHLY GRATED PARMESAN CHEESE, TO PASS AT THE TABLE

1. Heat the oil in the saucepan over medium heat. Add the onion, garlic, carrots and celery and cook, stirring occasionally, for about 10 minutes.

2. Stir in the parsley, basil, spaghetti sauce and stock and bring to a simmer. Add the pasta and cook, stirring often, until al dente, 7 to 10 minutes.

3. Taste and add salt and pepper, if needed. Serve in heavy pottery bowls. Pass the Parmesan at the table.

Italian Sausage Soup

Serve this with crusty bread and a melon salad.

5-quart stockpot
Makes 1 1/2 quarts/6 moderate servings

1 POUND MILD ITALIAN LINK SAUSAGE
1 TABLESPOON EXTRA-VIRGIN OLIVE OIL
2 YELLOW ONIONS, CHOPPED
1 GREEN BELL PEPPER, SEEDED AND DICED
2 GARLIC CLOVES, MINCED
1 QUART HOMEMADE BEEF STOCK OR CANNED BROTH
1 CUP DRY RED WINE
2 CUPS FRESH OR CANNED CHOPPED TOMATOES
1/4 CUP CHOPPED FRESH PARSLEY
1 TEASPOON CHOPPED FRESH BASIL (DO NOT USE DRIED. IF FRESH
   ISN'T AVAILABLE, LEAVE IT OUT.)
1 TEASPOON CHOPPED FRESH THYME, OR 1/2 TEASPOON DRIED
2 MEDIUM ZUCCHINI, SLICED
1 TABLESPOON PESTO (PAGE 43; OPTIONAL)
SALT AND PEPPER, TO TASTE
FRESHLY GRATED PARMESAN CHEESE, FOR SERVING

1. In the stockpot, cook the sausage over medium heat until browned. Remove and reserve. Pour off any rendered fat. Add the olive oil to the pot, along with the onions, bell pepper and garlic. Cook, with the lid slightly ajar, stirring now and then, until the vegetables are tender, 5 to 7 minutes.

2. Stir in the stock, wine, tomatoes and 1 cup of water. Slice the sausage into bite-size pieces and add to the pot. Cover and simmer for 30 minutes.

3. Skim off any fat that has risen to the top of the soup. (If there is time, chill the soup to solidify the fat, making it easier to remove. If the soup

is chilled, bring it back to a simmer before continuing.) Stir in the parsley, basil, thyme and zucchini and simmer, covered, until the zucchini is just tender, about 5 minutes.

4. Stir in the pesto, if using. Add salt and pepper to taste. Serve in flat soup plates. Pass the Parmesan at the table.

Martha's Sweet-and-Sour Cabbage Soup

Sweet-and-sour flavors are prevalent in Eastern European cookery. Martha Mervis of Danville, Illinois, who has a Polish-Russian heritage, gave me her cabbage soup recipe flavored with sugar and sour salt (citric acid). Martha uses the full amount of sugars and sours called for. I use about half. It can be adjusted to suit your particular taste.

5-quart stockpot
Makes 3 quarts/8 moderate servings

1½ POUNDS BEEF CHUCK, OR 2 POUNDS BEEF SHORT RIBS
2 QUARTS COLD WATER
2 CELERY RIBS WITH LEAVES, LEFT WHOLE
1 PARSNIP, PEELED AND LEFT WHOLE
1 LARGE YELLOW ONION, HALVED LENGTHWISE AND SLICED
2 CARROTS, THICKLY SLICED
4 FRESH PARSLEY SPRIGS
1 LARGE HEAD OF CABBAGE, COARSELY SHREDDED
1 TABLESPOON PLUS 1 TEASPOON SALT
BOILING WATER, AS NEEDED
1 CAN (14 OUNCES) WHOLE TOMATOES, BROKEN UP
1 CAN (10¾ OUNCES) CONDENSED TOMATO SOUP
1 SMALL APPLE, PEELED, QUARTERED, CORED AND SLICED
¼ CUP RAISINS

6 TO 12 TABLESPOONS SUGAR
4 TO 8 TABLESPOONS BROWN SUGAR
1½ TO 3 TEASPOONS CITRIC ACID (SOUR SALT)
SALT AND PEPPER, TO TASTE

1. Trim any excess fat from the beef. If using chuck, cut into bite-size pieces. Place the beef in the stockpot with the cold water and bring to a boil. Skim off the foam that rises to the top. Add the celery, parsnip, onion, carrots and parsley. Cover and cook at a simmer while preparing the cabbage (see Step 2).

2. Meanwhile, place the shredded cabbage in a large bowl and sprinkle with 1 tablespoon of the salt. Pour boiling water over the cabbage to cover; let stand for 10 minutes.

3. Drain the cabbage. Add it to the stockpot along with the tomatoes, tomato soup, apple, raisins and the remaining 1 teaspoon salt. Stir in half of the sugars and citric acid. Cover and simmer gently for 3 hours.

4. Taste the soup and adjust the sweet and sour flavor by adding more sugar or citric acid, to taste. Cover and cook for 1 hour more. Add salt and pepper, if needed.

5. When the soup is done, remove the parsnip, celery and parsley. If using short ribs, remove from the pot. Discard the bones and cut the meat into bite-size pieces. Return the meat to the pot. Serve in heavy bowls.

Ukrainian Borsch

This is a ruby red soup with a wonderful complex flavor that lets neither the beets nor the cabbage predominate.

3-quart and 2-quart saucepans
Makes 2 quarts/4 moderate servings

12 OUNCES LEAN BEEF BOTTOM ROUND OR ROUND, CUBED
1 QUART HOMEMADE BEEF STOCK OR CANNED BROTH
1 BAY LEAF
2 SMALL YELLOW ONIONS, PEELED, ONE STUCK WITH A WHOLE
   CLOVE, THE OTHER, CHOPPED
⅛ TEASPOON COARSELY GROUND PEPPER
1 TABLESPOON EXTRA–VIRGIN OLIVE OIL
1 CARROT, DICED
1 CELERY RIB, DICED
2 MEDIUM BEETS, PEELED AND DICED
2 MEDIUM RUSSET OR WHITE POTATOES, PEELED AND DICED
¼ MEDIUM HEAD OF CABBAGE, SHREDDED (ABOUT 8 OUNCES)
1 CAN (8 OUNCES) TOMATO SAUCE
1 TEASPOON CIDER VINEGAR
SALT AND PEPPER, TO TASTE
CHOPPED FRESH DILL OR PARSLEY, FOR GARNISH

1. Combine the beef, stock, bay leaf, the onion with a clove and the pepper in the larger saucepan. Bring to a boil; skim off any foam that rises. Reduce the heat to a simmer, cover and cook for 1½ hours. Remove the bay leaf and clove-studded onion.

2. After the beef and stock has cooked for 1½ hours, heat the oil over medium heat in the smaller saucepan. Add the chopped onion, carrot and celery and cook, stirring often, until the onion is tender, 5 to 7 minutes.

3. Add the vegetables to the soup, along with the beets, potatoes, cabbage, tomato sauce and vinegar. Cover and simmer for 1 hour, or until the meat and the vegetables are tender.

4. Add salt and pepper to taste. Serve in flat soup plates, sprinkled with fresh dill or parsley. Pass a cruet of vinegar so diners can add to their portion, if they wish.

Oxtail Barley Soup

Oxtails are extremely bony and covered with fat. By starting well in advance and chilling the stock to remove the congealed fat before proceeding with the soup itself, you can easily separate these offending parts from the flavorful broth.

5-quart stockpot
Makes 2 quarts/6 moderate servings

2 TABLESPOONS EXTRA-VIRGIN OLIVE OIL
2 OXTAILS, DISJOINTED (ABOUT 3 POUNDS)
2 QUARTS COLD WATER
1 TEASPOON SALT (OPTIONAL)
1 YELLOW ONION, UNPEELED AND QUARTERED
4 WHOLE PEPPERCORNS
1 BAY LEAF
1 WHOLE CLOVE
2 CARROTS, DICED
2 CELERY RIBS, DICED
1/2 CUP BARLEY
1 CAN (8 OUNCES) TOMATO SAUCE
1/2 TEASPOON CHOPPED FRESH THYME, OR 1/4 TEASPOON DRIED
1/2 CUP DRY WHITE WINE
PEPPER, TO TASTE

1. Heat the oil in the stockpot. Brown the oxtails in the oil, one layer at a time. Add the cold water and bring to a boil. Skim off any foam that rises. Stir in the salt, onion, peppercorns, bay leaf and clove. Bring to a simmer and cook, with the lid slightly ajar, for 4 hours.

2. Remove the oxtails from the pot. Strain the stock. Separate the meat from the oxtails and return it to the stock, discarding the fat and the bones. Chill overnight, or until the fat solidifies on the top of the stock.

3. Remove and discard the solidified fat from the stock. Bring the

stock to a simmer. Add the carrots, celery, barley, tomato sauce, thyme and wine. Cover and cook for 1 hour.

4. Taste and season with salt and pepper, if needed. Serve in flat soup plates.

K.C. Steak Soup

Walk into a restaurant in Kansas City and you'll find steak soup on the menu. It's as much a specialty as the steak itself. Thick and peppery—and addictive. Serve with a robust red wine and Steak House Rolls (page 199).

3-quart nonreactive saucepan and a large nonstick skillet
Makes 7 cups/4 moderate servings

3 TABLESPOONS UNSALTED BUTTER
1/4 CUP UNBLEACHED ALL-PURPOSE FLOUR
1 QUART HOMEMADE BEEF STOCK OR CANNED BROTH, HEATED
   UNTIL HOT
1 YELLOW ONION, FINELY CHOPPED
2 CARROTS, DICED
2 CELERY RIBS, DICED
1 CAN (8 OUNCES) TOMATO SAUCE
1/2 TEASPOON CHOPPED FRESH THYME, OR 1/4 TEASPOON DRIED
1 TEASPOON RED WINE VINEGAR
1 TEASPOON WORCESTERSHIRE SAUCE
1 TABLESPOON EXTRA-VIRGIN OLIVE OIL
1 POUND COARSELY GROUND STRIP OR ROUND STEAK★
SALT AND PEPPER, TO TASTE
CHOPPED FRESH PARSLEY, FOR GARNISH

★Cut the steak into cubes and grind in a food processor, or ask the butcher to grind it for you. Leftover grilled steak can be ground and used; just add it to the soup without pre-browning.

1. Melt the butter in the saucepan. Add the flour and cook over medium-low heat, stirring often, for 2 minutes. Add the hot stock and cook, stirring constantly, until the soup thickens. Stir in the onion, carrots, celery, tomato sauce, thyme, vinegar and Worcestershire. Bring to a simmer, cover and cook while preparing the meat.

2. Heat the olive oil in the nonstick skillet. Sauté the ground steak in the oil until browned. Add to the soup. Cover and simmer for 30 minutes.

3. Add salt and pepper to taste. Kansas City cooks add at least 1 teaspoon freshly ground pepper. If you're not from Kansas City, you may want less. Garnish the servings with the parsley.

Ham Vegetable Soup

This is old-fashioned good. Great family fare.

5-quart stockpot
Makes 2 ½ quarts/6 moderate servings

1 TEASPOON EXTRA-VIRGIN OLIVE OIL
1 YELLOW ONION, CHOPPED
1 ½ QUARTS COLD WATER
12 OUNCES COOKED HAM, DICED
2 TOMATOES, PEELED, SEEDED AND DICED
2 CELERY RIBS, DICED
2 CARROTS, DICED
1 CUP FRESH OR FROZEN BABY LIMA BEANS
1 CUP FRESH OR FROZEN GREEN PEAS
1 CUP FRESH OR FROZEN CORN KERNELS
¼ CUP CHOPPED FRESH PARSLEY
1 BAY LEAF
1 TEASPOON SUGAR
1 TEASPOON CIDER VINEGAR
SALT AND PEPPER, TO TASTE

1. Heat the oil in the stockpot over medium heat. Add the onion and cook, with the lid slightly ajar, until tender, 5 to 7 minutes.

2. Stir in the cold water, ham, tomatoes, celery, carrots, lima beans, peas, corn, parsley, bay leaf, sugar and vinegar. Cover and simmer for 45 minutes.

3. Taste and add salt and pepper, if needed. Serve in heavy pottery bowls.

Poor Man's Bouillabaisse

This is not a complicated bouillabaisse but it's very good. Since I'm too cheap to buy saffron, I add a dash of turmeric to the stock for color. Be sure to serve this with an ample basket of French bread.

3-quart nonreactive saucepan
Makes 2 quarts/4 moderate servings

½ CUP DRY WHITE WINE
1 CUP COLD WATER
2 CUPS BOTTLED CLAM JUICE
2 THIN LEMON SLICES
1 BAY LEAF
2 BLACK PEPPERCORNS
3 FRESH THYME SPRIGS, OR ½ TEASPOON DRIED
1 TABLESPOON EXTRA-VIRGIN OLIVE OIL
2 YELLOW ONIONS, THINLY SLICED
1 GARLIC CLOVE, MINCED
2 CUPS FRESH OR CANNED CHOPPED TOMATOES
3 TABLESPOONS CHOPPED FRESH PARSLEY
½ TEASPOON TURMERIC
1 TABLESPOON CHOPPED FRESH FENNEL LEAVES, OR 3 FENNEL SEEDS, CRUSHED

1½ POUNDS MIXED, SHELLED, FRESH, FROZEN OR CANNED
   SHELLFISH (CHOOSE FROM CRAB, LOBSTER, SHRIMP AND CLAMS)
SALT AND HOT PEPPER SAUCE, TO TASTE

1. In the saucepan, combine the wine, cold water, clam juice, lemon slices, bay leaf, peppercorns and thyme. Simmer, partially covered, for 15 minutes. Strain, reserving the stock.

2. In the rinsed and dried pot, warm the olive oil over medium heat. Add the onions and garlic and cook, with the lid slightly ajar, for 5 to 7 minutes, or until the onions are tender.

3. Stir in the reserved stock, the tomatoes, parsley, turmeric and fennel. Cover and simmer for 15 minutes.

4. Add the shellfish and cook for 5 to 10 minutes longer, or until the fish is opaque. Add salt and hot pepper sauce to taste. Serve in flat soup plates.

Selma's Lentil Soup

My good friend Selma Young invited my husband and me to dinner and apologized for serving only soup. We were so pleased, I asked for her recipe.

5-quart stockpot
Makes 3 1/2 quarts/10 moderate servings

2 TABLESPOONS CANOLA OIL
1 YELLOW ONION, CHOPPED
3 SKINNY CARROTS, THINLY SLICED
1 CELERY RIB, DICED
1/2 GREEN BELL PEPPER, SEEDED AND DICED
2 GARLIC CLOVES, MINCED
1 POUND LENTILS, RINSED AND DRAINED
2 QUARTS HOMEMADE BEEF STOCK OR CANNED BROTH
1 QUART COLD WATER
1/4 CUP TOMATO KETCHUP
2 TABLESPOONS RED WINE VINEGAR
1 TEASPOON CHOPPED FRESH THYME, OR 1/2 TEASPOON DRIED
3/4 TEASPOON POWDERED MUSTARD
1 BAY LEAF
1/2 CUP DRY RED WINE
SALT AND PEPPER, TO TASTE

1. Heat the oil in the stockpot over medium heat. Stir in the onion, carrots, celery, bell pepper and garlic. Cook, with the lid slightly ajar, stirring often, until the vegetables are tender, 5 to 7 minutes.

2. Add the lentils, stock, cold water, ketchup, vinegar, thyme, powdered mustard and bay leaf. Cover and simmer for 1 1/2 hours.

3. Discard the bay leaf. Add the wine. Cover and simmer for 15 minutes longer. Taste and add salt and pepper, if needed. Serve in flat soup plates.

Fruited Lentil and Rice Soup

Cumin gives this a Middle Eastern flavor. Leftover roast lamb can be cubed and added to the finished soup, but it is good just as it is.

5-quart stockpot
Makes 2½ quarts/6 moderate servings

2 TABLESPOONS EXTRA-VIRGIN OLIVE OIL
1 YELLOW ONION, CHOPPED
1 GARLIC CLOVE, MINCED
2 CARROTS, DICED
2 CELERY RIBS, DICED
½ GREEN BELL PEPPER, SEEDED AND DICED
2 QUARTS HOMEMADE BEEF STOCK OR CANNED BROTH
1 CUP LENTILS, RINSED AND DRAINED
½ CUP BASMATI RICE
1 TOMATO, PEELED, SEEDED AND DICED
1 TABLESPOON CHOPPED FRESH PARSLEY
1 TABLESPOON FRESH LEMON JUICE
½ CUP GOLDEN RAISINS
¼ CUP SNIPPED DRIED APRICOTS (½-INCH PIECES)
1 TEASPOON GROUND CUMIN
SALT AND PEPPER, TO TASTE

1. Heat the oil in the stockpot. Add the onion, garlic, carrots, celery and bell pepper and cook, with the lid slightly ajar, stirring now and then, until the onion is tender, 5 to 7 minutes.

2. Add the stock, lentils, rice, tomato, parsley and lemon juice. Cover and simmer for 45 minutes.

3. Stir in the raisins, apricots and cumin. Cover and simmer for 15 minutes, or until the lentils and rice are tender.

4. Taste and add salt and pepper, if desired. Serve in flat soup plates.

Beer Garden Pea Soup

Your first thought may be to enjoy this with a beer, and that's very good, but it's even better with a full-bodied, medium-dry white wine such as a Rhine. Spread pumpernickel bread with a butter-mustard mixture to serve on the side.

5-quart stockpot
Makes 3 quarts/8 moderate servings

1 POUND GREEN SPLIT PEAS, RINSED AND DRAINED
2 TABLESPOONS EXTRA-VIRGIN OLIVE OIL
2 YELLOW ONIONS, FINELY CHOPPED
2 CARROTS, DICED
2 CELERY RIBS, DICED
5 CUPS COLD WATER
1 CAN (12 OUNCES) BEER
1 MEATY HAM BONE (ABOUT 1 POUND)
1 MEDIUM RUSSET OR WHITE POTATO, PEELED AND DICED
1/4 CUP CHOPPED FRESH PARSLEY
1 TEASPOON CHOPPED FRESH THYME, OR 1/2 TEASPOON DRIED
1/2 TEASPOON POWDERED MUSTARD
1 TABLESPOON CIDER VINEGAR
8 OUNCES FULLY-COOKED BRATWURST LINKS, SLICED DIAGONALLY
SALT AND PEPPER, TO TASTE

1. Combine the split peas with 1 1/2 quarts of water and soak for 6 to 8 hours or overnight. Alternately, bring the water to a boil, add the peas, and boil for 2 minutes. Remove from the heat, cover and let stand for 1 hour.

2. Heat the oil in the stockpot over medium heat. Add the onions, carrots and celery and cook, stirring often, until the onions are tender, 5 to 7 minutes.

3. Add the cold water, beer, ham bone, potato, parsley, thyme,

powdered mustard and vinegar. Drain the soaked peas and add to the pot. Bring to a boil. Reduce the heat to a simmer, cover and cook, stirring now and then, until the peas are very tender, 3 to 4 hours.

4. Remove the ham bone. When cool enough to handle, remove any lean ham from the bone and return it to the pot. Discard the fat and the bone. Add the bratwurst slices and heat through. Taste and add salt and pepper, if desired. Serve in flat soup plates.

Hoppin' John Soup

Hoppin' John, made with black-eyed peas and rice, is eaten in the South on New Year's Day to bring good luck during the following year. I use brown rice, rather than white, and make my good luck into a tasty soup. It's good with corn bread.

3-quart saucepan
Makes 1 1/2 quarts/4 moderate servings

1 CUP DRIED BLACK-EYED PEAS, RINSED AND DRAINED
1 TABLESPOON CANOLA OIL
1 YELLOW ONION, CHOPPED
2 GARLIC CLOVES, MINCED
3 CARROTS, CHOPPED
2 CELERY RIBS WITH LEAVES, CHOPPED
1 QUART HOMEMADE CHICKEN STOCK OR CANNED BROTH
1/3 CUP UNCOOKED BROWN RICE
2 TABLESPOONS CHOPPED FRESH PARSLEY
1 TEASPOON CHOPPED FRESH THYME, OR 1/2 TEASPOON DRIED
1 TEASPOON CHOPPED FRESH WINTER SAVORY, OR 1/4 TEASPOON DRIED
1/8 TEASPOON CRUSHED RED PEPPER FLAKES
1/8 TEASPOON CELERY SEEDS
SALT AND PEPPER, TO TASTE

1. Combine the peas with 3 cups of water and soak for 6 to 8 hours or overnight. Alternately, bring the water to a boil, add the peas, and boil for 2 minutes. Remove from the heat, cover and let stand for 1 hour.

2. Heat the oil in the saucepan over medium heat. Add the onion, garlic, carrots and celery and cook, with the lid slightly ajar, stirring now and then, until the onion is tender, 5 to 7 minutes.

3. Drain the soaked peas and add to the pot. Add the stock, rice, parsley, thyme, savory, pepper flakes and celery seeds. Cover and simmer for 1 hour, or until the peas are tender.

4. Taste and add salt and pepper, if needed. Serve in pottery bowls.

Black Bean Soup

For this colorful soup the beans are simmered in a vegetable-filled broth. It's different from the usual puree.

3-quart saucepan
Makes 2½ quarts/6 moderate servings

1 CUP DRIED BLACK OR TURTLE BEANS, RINSED AND DRAINED

1 TABLESPOON EXTRA–VIRGIN OLIVE OIL

1 LARGE YELLOW ONION, CHOPPED

3 GARLIC CLOVES, MINCED

1 QUART HOMEMADE BEEF STOCK OR CANNED BROTH

4 CARROTS, SLICED

4 TOMATOES, PEELED, SEEDED AND CHOPPED

1 GREEN BELL PEPPER, SEEDED AND DICED

1 RED BELL PEPPER, SEEDED AND DICED

2 TABLESPOONS CHOPPED FRESH PARSLEY

1 TABLESPOON CHOPPED FRESH THYME, OR 1 TEASPOON DRIED

1 TABLESPOON RED WINE VINEGAR

½ TEASPOON POWDERED MUSTARD

¼ TEASPOON CRUSHED RED PEPPER FLAKES

SALT AND PEPPER, TO TASTE

1. Combine the beans with 3 cups of water and soak for 6 to 8 hours or overnight. Alternately, bring the water to a boil, add the beans and boil for 2 minutes. Remove from the heat, cover and let stand for 1 hour.

2. Heat the oil in the saucepan over medium heat. Add the onion and garlic and cook, stirring now and then, until the onion is tender, 5 to 7 minutes.

3. Drain the soaked peas and add to the pot, along with the stock. Bring to a boil. Reduce the heat to a simmer, cover and cook for 1 hour.

4. Stir in the carrots, tomatoes, bell peppers, parsley, thyme, vinegar, powdered mustard and pepper flakes. Cover and simmer for 1 hour.

5. Add salt and pepper to taste. Serve in heavy pottery bowls.

Basque Bean Soup

This soup can be made with or without the chicken wings—it's good either way. Serve with an assortment of homemade breads.

5-quart stockpot
Makes 2½ quarts (without the chicken wings)/6 moderate servings

1 CUP DRIED GREAT NORTHERN BEANS, RINSED AND DRAINED
1 TABLESPOON EXTRA-VIRGIN OLIVE OIL
1 LARGE YELLOW ONION, CHOPPED
1 GARLIC CLOVE, MINCED
3 CUPS COLD WATER
1 QUART HOMEMADE CHICKEN STOCK OR CANNED BROTH
2 POUNDS CHICKEN WINGS (OPTIONAL)
1 TABLESPOON CHOPPED FRESH OREGANO, OR 1 TEASPOON DRIED
1 TABLESPOON CHOPPED FRESH MARJORAM, OR 1 TEASPOON DRIED
½ HEAD OF CABBAGE, COARSELY SHREDDED
SALT AND PEPPER, TO TASTE

1. Combine the beans with 3 cups of water and soak for 6 to 8 hours or overnight. Alternately, bring the water to a boil, add the beans and boil for 2 minutes. Remove from the heat, cover and let stand for 1 hour.

2. Heat the oil in the stockpot over medium heat. Add the onion and the garlic and cook, stirring often, until the onion is tender, 5 to 7 minutes.

3. Drain the beans and add, along with the cold water. Bring to a boil. Reduce the heat to a simmer, cover and cook for 1 ½ hours.

4. Stir in the stock, chicken wings, oregano, marjoram and cabbage. Cover and simmer for 45 minutes.

5. Add salt and pepper to taste. Serve in flat soup plates.

Ham and White Bean Soup

This is an easy bean soup to make. After soaking the beans, simply put everything in the pot at once and cook until done. The working cook can make it one evening to serve the next.

3-quart saucepan
Makes 1 ½ quarts/4 moderate servings

1 CUP DRIED NAVY BEANS, RINSED AND DRAINED
1 ½ QUARTS HOMEMADE HAM STOCK OR WATER, HEATED UNTIL HOT
8 OUNCES HAM, DICED
1 SMALL YELLOW ONION, THINLY SLICED
1 BAY LEAF
1 TEASPOON CHOPPED FRESH THYME, OR ½ TEASPOON DRIED
SALT AND PEPPER, TO TASTE

1. Combine the beans with 3 cups of water and soak for 6 to 8 hours or overnight. Alternately, bring the water to a boil, add the beans and boil for 2 minutes. Remove from the heat, cover and let stand for 1 hour.

2. Drain the soaked beans and place in the saucepan. Add the ham stock or water, ham, onion, bay leaf and thyme. Bring to a boil. Reduce the heat to a simmer, cover and cook for 3 hours, or until the beans are tender.

3. Remove the bay leaf. Add salt and pepper, to taste. (If made ahead, wait until reheated to season with salt and pepper.) Mash some of the beans, or puree part of the soup in a blender or food processor, if you wish. Serve in heavy pottery bowls.

Yellow Pea Soup

This is an all-vegetable, high-fiber soup. Serve with crusty bread and fresh fruit.

5-quart stockpot
Makes 2 1/2 quarts/8 moderate servings

2 TABLESPOONS EXTRA-VIRGIN OLIVE OIL
1 MEDIUM YELLOW ONION, CHOPPED
3 CARROTS, DICED
2 CELERY RIBS, DICED
7 CUPS HOMEMADE HAM STOCK OR WATER, HEATED UNTIL HOT
1 POUND DRIED SPLIT YELLOW PEAS, RINSED IN HOT WATER AND DRAINED
1/4 CUP CHOPPED FRESH PARSLEY
2 TEASPOONS CHOPPED FRESH THYME, OR 1 TEASPOON DRIED
1 BAY LEAF
1 SMALL ONION STUCK WITH 2 WHOLE CLOVES
SALT AND PEPPER, TO TASTE

1. Heat the oil in the stockpot over medium heat. Add the chopped onion, carrots and celery and cook, stirring now and then, until the onion is tender, 5 to 7 minutes.

2. Add the hot ham stock or water, the peas, parsley, thyme, bay leaf and the onion stuck with cloves. Bring to a boil. Reduce the heat to a simmer, cover and cook for 1 hour.

3. Remove the bay leaf and the clove-studded onion. Simmer, covered, for 1 hour, or until the peas are very tender.

4. Add salt and pepper to taste. Serve in heavy pottery bowls.

Savory Stews

With stick-to-your-ribs goodness

Here are the old-fashioned favorites you love to come home to—hearty combinations of meats and vegetables, flavored with herbs and sauced with savory gravies. Cooked on stovetop or simmered in the oven, they are home-style eating at its best.

Ratatouille

Ratatouille is a marvelous all-vegetable stew, featuring eggplant, zucchini and tomatoes. It requires a rather large casserole or pot for layering the ingredients, but it cooks down to less than half the original volume. Serve with crusty bread and a variety of cheeses. Leftovers can be served cold as a salad or side dish.

5-quart stovetop-to-oven casserole or stockpot
Makes 2 quarts/6 moderate servings

6 TABLESPOONS EXTRA-VIRGIN OLIVE OIL
2 YELLOW ONIONS, THINLY SLICED
2 GARLIC CLOVES, MINCED
1 EGGPLANT, PEELED AND CUBED
3 SMALL OR 2 MEDIUM ZUCCHINI, SLICED
1 RED BELL PEPPER, SEEDED AND CUT INTO STRIPS
4 RED-RIPE TOMATOES, PEELED AND SLICED
¼ CUP COARSELY CHOPPED FRESH BASIL (DO NOT USE DRIED)
1 TABLESPOON CHOPPED FRESH OREGANO, OR 1 TEASPOON DRIED
1 TEASPOON SALT
¼ TEASPOON PEPPER

1. Preheat the oven to 300°F. Warm 3 tablespoons of the oil in the casserole over medium heat. Remove from the heat. Layer the vegetables in the casserole, using half of each vegetable in each of two layers. Sprinkle the layers with the basil, oregano, salt and pepper, until all are used. Sprinkle the remaining 3 tablespoons oil over the top.

2. Cover and bake for 1 hour. Alternately, use a heavy stockpot, cover and simmer very gently on stovetop for 1 hour, using a wooden spoon to gently move the contents from time to time, but without actually stirring.

3. Uncover the casserole and gently move the contents with a wooden spoon so that they settle. Simmer, uncovered, on stovetop for 10 to 15 minutes to thicken the sauce. Serve in flat soup plates.

My Easy Minestrone

Don't tell anyone how really simple this is. Let them think you have slaved for hours. As with most minestrones, this is even better the second day. Use stock, broth or water, according to your taste buds.

5-quart stockpot and a nonstick skillet
Makes 2 1/2 quarts/6 generous servings

6 CUPS ANY KIND OF STOCK, BROTH OR PLAIN WATER
4 CUPS COARSELY CHOPPED CABBAGE (ABOUT 1/2 HEAD)
2 CARROTS, COARSELY CHOPPED
1 YELLOW ONION, FINELY CHOPPED
1 CAN (8 OUNCES) TOMATO SAUCE
1 CAN (14- TO 16-OUNCES) WHITE OR LIGHT RED KIDNEY BEANS
   (WHITE KIDNEY BEANS ARE SOMETIMES CALLED CANNELLINI)
1 TABLESPOON CHOPPED FRESH OREGANO, OR 1 TEASPOON DRIED
8 OUNCES ITALIAN LINK SAUSAGES
2 MEDIUM ZUCCHINI, SLICED
4 OUNCES SPAGHETTI, BROKEN
SALT AND PEPPER, TO TASTE
FRESHLY GRATED PARMESAN CHEESE, TO PASS AT THE TABLE

1. Combine the stock, cabbage, carrots, onion, tomato sauce, kidney beans and oregano in the stockpot. Simmer, covered, until the vegetables are tender, 10 to 15 minutes.

2. While the pot bubbles, cut the sausage into bite-size chunks. Sauté the sausage in the nonstick skillet until cooked through and browned. Use a slotted spoon to transfer the browned meat to the pot, leaving the rendered fat behind.

3. Add the zucchini and spaghetti to the soup and cook, stirring occasionally, until both are tender, 7 to 10 minutes. Taste and add salt and pepper if needed. Serve in heavy bowls. Pass the Parmesan.

Moore's Meatless Minestrone

This is a stew to grow strong on! The rice in the mix "cooks up," thickening the sauce without the usual macaroni.

5-quart stockpot
Makes 3 quarts/6 generous servings

1 PACKAGE (ABOUT 1 CUP) MOORE'S MINESTRONE MIX (RECIPE
FOLLOWS), RINSED AND DRAINED
1 TABLESPOON EXTRA-VIRGIN OLIVE OIL
2 GARLIC CLOVES, MINCED
2 YELLOW ONIONS, CHOPPED
2 QUARTS HOMEMADE BEEF OR VEGETABLE STOCK OR CANNED
BROTH
2 TABLESPOONS TOMATO PASTE
2 CUPS CHOPPED FRESH OR CANNED TOMATOES
2 CUPS CHOPPED CABBAGE (ABOUT ¼ HEAD)
2 CELERY RIBS, COARSELY CHOPPED
2 CARROTS, COARSELY CHOPPED
1 CUP COARSELY CHOPPED GREEN BEANS, ROMA PREFERRED
1 ZUCCHINI, SLICED
1 TABLESPOON CHOPPED FRESH BASIL (DO NOT USE DRIED. IF FRESH
IS NOT AVAILABLE, LEAVE IT OUT.)
1 TABLESPOON CHOPPED ITALIAN FLAT-LEAF PARSLEY
1 TABLESPOON CHOPPED FRESH OREGANO, OR ½ TEASPOON DRIED
SALT AND PEPPER, TO TASTE
FRESHLY GRATED PARMESAN CHEESE, FOR SERVING

1. Combine the minestrone mix with 3 cups of water and soak for
6 to 8 hours or overnight. Alternately, bring the water to a boil, add the
minestrone mix and boil for 2 minutes. Cover and let stand for 1 hour.
Drain, discarding the soaking water.

2. Warm the oil in the stockpot over medium heat. Add the garlic
and the onions and cook, stirring often, until the onions are tender, 5 to 7
minutes. Add the stock and the drained minestrone mix and bring to a
gentle boil. Reduce the heat to a simmer, cover and cook until the beans
are tender, 2 to 3 hours.

3. Stir a little of the soup into the tomato paste and stir the mixture
into the soup. Add the tomatoes, cabbage, celery, carrots, green beans,

zucchini, basil, parsley and oregano. Cover and simmer until the vegetables are tender, 30 to 45 minutes.

4. Taste and add salt and pepper, if desired. Serve in flat soup plates. A spoonful of Parmesan cheese can be stirred into each serving or it can be offered at the table.

Moore's Minestrone Mix

This has a long shelf life, making it easy to keep on hand.

no-cook
Makes 12 packages

1 POUND DRIED NAVY BEANS
1 POUND DRIED PINTO BEANS
1 POUND DRIED GREEN SPLIT PEAS
1 POUND DRIED BROWN LENTILS
1 POUND BARLEY
1 POUND BROWN RICE

1. Stir together all of the ingredients taking care to mix thoroughly. Spoon 1 cup of the mix into each of 12 individual sealable plastic sacks. Divide any extra mix equally among the sacks before closing.

Polish Bigos

This was originally a hunter's stew, using game as well as sausage, but I make mine with just the sausage.

3-quart saucepan
Makes 2 quarts/8 moderate servings

12 OUNCES KIELBASA OR POLISH SAUSAGE
1 TABLESPOON EXTRA-VIRGIN OLIVE OIL
1 LARGE YELLOW ONION, CHOPPED
1 LARGE GRANNY SMITH APPLE, PEELED, CORED, QUARTERED AND
  SLICED
2 CUPS HOMEMADE CHICKEN STOCK OR CANNED BROTH
1 CUP COLD WATER
2 CUPS CHOPPED FRESH OR CANNED TOMATOES
2 CUPS (1 POUND) FRESH SAUERKRAUT, RINSED IN HOT WATER
  AND DRAINED
1 TABLESPOON ALL-PURPOSE FLOUR
1 TABLESPOON SUGAR
BOILED POTATOES, FOR SERVING

1. Place the sausage in the saucepan, add water to cover and bring to a simmer. Cover and simmer for 30 minutes. Remove the sausage; rinse and dry the pot. (If the sausage is sold fully cooked, skip this step.)

2. Heat the oil in the saucepan over medium heat. Add the onion and the apple and cook, stirring often, until the onion is tender, 5 to 7 minutes.

3. Add the stock, cold water, tomatoes and sauerkraut. Slice the cooked sausage and add to the pot. Stir the flour and the sugar together and stir into the pot. Cover and simmer for 1 hour.

4. Taste and add salt and pepper, if needed. Place 1 or 2 boiled potatoes in each bowl and ladle the stew over the potatoes.

Pork and Potato Stew

Both sweet and white potatoes flavor this stew. It's good with a sweet-sour dressed spinach salad.

3-quart saucepan
Makes 1½ quarts/4 moderate servings

2 TABLESPOONS EXTRA-VIRGIN OLIVE OIL
1 YELLOW ONION, CHOPPED
1 GARLIC CLOVE, MINCED
1 POUND LEAN PORK LOIN, CUBED
2 CUPS HOMEMADE BEEF STOCK OR CANNED BROTH
1 MEDIUM RUSSET OR WHITE POTATO, PEELED AND CUBED
1 SWEET POTATO, PEELED AND CUBED
1 CUP FRESH OR FROZEN CORN KERNELS
1 LARGE TOMATO, PEELED, SEEDED AND CHOPPED
½ TEASPOON FRESH ROSEMARY LEAVES, OR ¼ TEASPOON DRIED
SALT AND PEPPER, TO TASTE
2 TABLESPOONS CORNSTARCH
¼ CUP COLD WATER

1. Warm the oil in the saucepan over medium heat. Add the onion and garlic and cook, stirring often, until the onion is tender, 5 to 7 minutes. Remove with a slotted spoon and reserve.

2. Add the pork to the pot and cook, stirring now and then, until the meat no longer is pink. Return the onion and garlic to the pot, add the stock and 1 cup of water. Simmer, covered, for 30 minutes.

3. Stir in the potato, sweet potato, corn, tomato and rosemary. Cover and simmer until the potatoes are tender, about 30 minutes. Taste and add salt and pepper, if needed.

4. Stir the cornstarch into the cold water and then stir the mixture into the stew. Cook, stirring constantly, just until thickened, about 3 minutes. Serve in heavy pottery bowls.

Porcupine Stew

The rice pokes out as the stew cooks, giving the meatballs their quaint name. Good served with coleslaw.

Makes 1½ quarts/4 moderate servings

1 RECIPE PORCUPINES (RECIPE FOLLOWS)
1 CAN (8 OUNCES) TOMATO SAUCE
¼ CUP DRY WHITE WINE
2 LARGE TOMATOES, PEELED, SEEDED AND CHOPPED
½ TEASPOON CHILI POWDER
FRESH ROSEMARY SPRIGS, FOR GARNISH

1. Preheat the oven to 350°F. Place the porcupines in a low-sided 2-quart casserole or nonreactive baking dish. Combine the tomato sauce, wine, tomatoes and chili powder. Pour over the meatballs, coating completely with the sauce.

2. Cover the dish and bake for 1 hour. Garnish the servings with sprigs of fresh rosemary.

Porcupines

Makes 16 meatballs

1 POUND LEAN GROUND BEEF
1 SMALL GARLIC CLOVE, MINCED
1 TEASPOON CHOPPED FRESH ROSEMARY, OR ¼ TEASPOON DRIED
¼ TEASPOON SALT
⅓ CUP UNCOOKED LONG-GRAIN RICE
1 LARGE EGG

1. Mix all of the ingredients together. Shape into sixteen 1-inch balls.

Savory Beef Stew

You may think of stew as family fare, but I serve this to company. It's good with chunky applesauce. Finish off dinner with brownies à la mode.

3-quart saucepan
Makes 1 1/2 quarts/4 moderate servings

2 TABLESPOONS PLUS 1 TEASPOON EXTRA-VIRGIN OLIVE OIL
1 LARGE YELLOW ONION, CHOPPED
1 POUND LEAN ROUND STEAK, CUBED
3 TABLESPOONS ALL-PURPOSE FLOUR
2 CUPS HOMEMADE BEEF STOCK OR CANNED BROTH, HEATED UNTIL HOT
3 CARROTS, SLICED DIAGONALLY
3 CELERY RIBS, SLICED DIAGONALLY
1 TABLESPOON CHOPPED FRESH PARSLEY
1 TABLESPOON TOMATO KETCHUP
1 TEASPOON FRESH LEMON JUICE
1 TEASPOON WORCESTERSHIRE SAUCE
1 TEASPOON CHOPPED FRESH WINTER SAVORY, OR 1/4 TEASPOON DRIED
1 TEASPOON CHOPPED FRESH MARJORAM, OR 1/2 TEASPOON DRIED
1/2 TEASPOON PREPARED MUSTARD
SALT AND PEPPER, TO TASTE
HOT COOKED BASMATI RICE OR STEAMED NEW POTATOES, FOR SERVING

1. Heat 1 teaspoon of the oil in the saucepan over medium heat. Add the onion and cook, stirring often, until tender, 5 to 7 minutes. Remove the onion with a slotted spoon and reserve.

2. Add the remaining 2 tablespoons oil to the pan. Roll the meat in the flour to coat. Add the meat to the pan and brown on all sides. Stir in any remaining flour.

3. Stir in the hot stock. Return the onion to the pot and stir in the carrots, celery, parsley, ketchup, lemon juice, Worcestershire, savory, marjoram and mustard. Cover and simmer for 1½ hours, or until the meat is tender.

4. Add salt and pepper, to taste. Serve over hot cooked rice or steamed new potatoes.

Old-Fashioned Beef Stew

For a family gathering, serve this Old-Fashioned Beef Stew with a choice of salads and desserts.

5-quart stockpot
Makes 2½ quarts/8 moderate servings

2 POUNDS LEAN BEEF BOTTOM ROUND OR ROUND, CUBED
3 TABLESPOONS ALL-PURPOSE FLOUR
3 TABLESPOONS EXTRA-VIRGIN OLIVE OIL
2 TEASPOONS SALT (OPTIONAL)
¼ TEASPOON PEPPER
16 PEARL ONIONS, PEELED AND LEFT WHOLE
8 SKINNY CARROTS, SLICED
4 MEDIUM RUSSET OR WHITE POTATOES, PEELED AND DICED
2 MEDIUM TURNIPS, PEELED AND DICED
2 CELERY RIBS, DICED
CHOPPED FRESH PARSLEY, FOR GARNISH

1. Toss the beef cubes in the flour to coat. Heat the oil in the stockpot over medium heat. Add the beef and brown on all sides. Stir in any flour that remains. Stir in the salt, pepper and 6 cups of water. Bring to a simmer. Cover and cook for 1 hour.

2. Stir in the onions, carrots, potatoes, turnips and celery. Cover and simmer for 1 hour.

3. Serve in flat soup plates. Garnish with the chopped parsley.

Yogurt-Beef Stroganoff

This is a good dish for entertaining. The meat sauce can be made the day before the party, to be reheated while you assemble a salad and cook the noodles.

large skillet and a covered casserole
Makes 1 1/2 quarts sauce/8 moderate servings

1 TABLESPOON EXTRA-VIRGIN OLIVE OIL

1 1/2 POUNDS LEAN BEEF SIRLOIN, CUT ACROSS THE GRAIN INTO THIN STRIPS

4 TABLESPOONS UNSALTED BUTTER

1 YELLOW ONION, CHOPPED

8 OUNCES BUTTON MUSHROOMS, SLICED

1/4 CUP ALL-PURPOSE FLOUR

2 CUPS HOMEMADE BEEF STOCK OR CANNED BROTH, HEATED UNTIL HOT

1 CUP PLAIN NONFAT YOGURT

1 1/2 TABLESPOONS TOMATO KETCHUP

1 1/2 TABLESPOONS PREPARED MUSTARD

1 1/2 TABLESPOONS WORCESTERSHIRE SAUCE

SALT AND PEPPER, TO TASTE

1 POUND WIDE NOODLES, COOKED ACCORDING TO PACKAGE INSTRUCTIONS

CHOPPED FRESH PARSLEY, FOR GARNISH

1. Heat the oil in the skillet over medium heat. Add half of the beef and cook, turning once, until it loses its red color. Transfer the meat to the casserole as it browns. Cook the remaining beef.

2. In the rinsed and dried skillet, melt the butter over medium heat. Add the onion and mushrooms and cook, stirring often, until tender. Sprinkle the flour over the mushrooms and the onions and stir in the hot stock. Cook, stirring, for 2 minutes; remove from the heat.

3. Stir together the yogurt, ketchup, mustard and Worcestershire. Stir the mixture into the stock; taste and add salt and pepper, if needed. Pour the sauce over the meat in the casserole. (The recipe may be made up to this point and the casserole refrigerated overnight.)

4. Preheat the oven to 350°F. When hot, bake the covered casserole for 30 minutes. (The refrigerated casserole may take up to 15 minutes longer.)

5. Serve over the hot cooked noodles. Sprinkle the servings with the chopped parsley.

Hungarian Goulash

Hungarian goulash, according to *Larousse Gastronomique,* "should not include flour or wine, nor should soured cream be added just before serving." It also suggests that the fat used to sauté the beef and onions be pork fat or lard. I break two of these rules. Canola oil replaces the lard (who cooks with lard these days?) and I use a small amount of flour to thicken the gravy, thereby shortening the usual cooking time. The flavoring, of course, is Hungarian paprika.

5-quart stockpot
Makes 2 1/2 quarts/6 moderate servings

3 TABLESPOONS CANOLA OIL

3 YELLOW ONIONS, QUARTERED

2 GARLIC CLOVES, SLICED

1 1/2 POUNDS LEAN BEEF BOTTOM ROUND OR ROUND, CUBED

2 TABLESPOONS ALL–PURPOSE FLOUR

1 TABLESPOON SWEET HUNGARIAN PAPRIKA

2 CUPS HOMEMADE BEEF STOCK, OR CANNED BROTH, HEATED UNTIL HOT

1 CUP HOT WATER

3 TOMATOES, PEELED, SEEDED AND COARSELY CHOPPED

3 MEDIUM RUSSET OR WHITE POTATOES, PEELED AND COARSELY
  CHOPPED
½ SMALL HEAD OF CABBAGE, COARSELY CHOPPED
2 TABLESPOONS CHOPPED FRESH PARSLEY
1 TEASPOON CARAWAY SEEDS
¼ TEASPOON CELERY SEEDS
SALT AND PEPPER, TO TASTE

1. Heat the oil in the stockpot over medium heat. Add the onions
and garlic and cook, stirring often, for 5 minutes. Add the beef cubes and
cook, stirring, until all pink color is gone. Remove from the heat.

2. Sprinkle on the flour and paprika. Stir in the hot stock and hot
water. Return to the heat and simmer, covered, for 1 hour.

3. Stir in the tomatoes, potatoes, cabbage, parsley, caraway seeds
and celery seeds. Cover and simmer for 1 hour, or until the meat is tender.

4. Add salt and pepper to taste. Serve in flat soup plates.

Stacked Irish Stew

This couldn't be easier. Layer the ingredients in the pot and simmer to
perfection.

5-quart stockpot or dutch oven
Makes 2 quarts/6 moderate servings

2 POUNDS BONELESS LAMB SHOULDER OR LEG, CUBED
4 YELLOW ONIONS, SLICED
6 MEDIUM RUSSET OR WHITE POTATOES, PEELED AND SLICED
⅓ CUP CHOPPED FRESH PARSLEY
2 TEASPOONS SALT (OPTIONAL)
¼ TEASPOON GROUND PEPPER
2 CUPS COLD WATER

1. Using half of each, layer the lamb, onions, potatoes and parsley in the stockpot, layering them in the order listed. Sprinkle with half of the salt and pepper. Repeat the layering and use the remaining salt and pepper.

2. Pour the cold water into the pot. Slowly bring to a boil. Reduce the heat to a simmer, cover and cook, for 3 hours, or until the potatoes begin to break apart. Alternately, cook, covered, in a 300°F oven for 3 hours. Serve in flat soup plates.

Lamb Stew with Apricots

Lamb with dried fruit is an intriguing combination. The lemon juice provides the perfect balance for the sweetness of the apricots. Good with a mushroom-spinach salad.

5-quart stockpot or casserole
Makes 1¼ quarts/4 moderate servings

1 TABLESPOON EXTRA-VIRGIN OLIVE OIL
1 TABLESPOON UNSALTED BUTTER
2 YELLOW ONIONS, SLICED
2 POUNDS BONELESS LAMB SHOULDER OR LEG, CUBED
2 CUPS HOT WATER
2 TABLESPOONS CHOPPED FRESH PARSLEY OR CORIANDER
1 TEASPOON SALT (OPTIONAL)
¼ TEASPOON COARSELY GROUND BLACK PEPPER
½ TEASPOON GROUND GINGER
⅛ TEASPOON GROUND CINNAMON
1½ CUPS DRIED APRICOTS
1 TABLESPOON FRESH LEMON JUICE
COOKED COUSCOUS OR BROWN RICE, FOR SERVING
CHOPPED FRESH PARSLEY OR CORIANDER, FOR GARNISH

1. Heat the oil and butter in the stockpot over medium–high heat until the butter melts. Add the onions and cook, stirring constantly, until tender, about 4 minutes. Add the lamb and cook, stirring often, until the pieces lose all pink color. Stir in the hot water, parsley, salt, pepper, ginger and cinnamon. (If using the coriander, don't add it until you add the apricots.) Simmer, covered, for 1 hour. Alternately bake in a 350°F oven for 1 hour.

2. Stir in the apricots, lemon juice and coriander (if using). Cover and simmer or bake for 20 minutes, or until the lamb is tender and the apricots are soft.

3. Serve with couscous or rice. Garnish the servings with chopped fresh parsley or coriander.

Brunswick Stew

Brunswick stew was originally a hunter's specialty, combining succotash vegetables with freshly caught squirrel or rabbit. The non–hunter, like myself, uses chicken from the grocer's meat case. Some recipes advise cooking the stew until it turns to mush. I like mine short of that.

There is an ongoing, albeit friendly, argument between the residents of Brunswick County, Virginia, and those of Brunswick, Georgia, about the origins of Brunswick Stew. Each claims to be its inventor. The question will never be resolved—it's one man's word against another's. In the meantime, we can all enjoy a good mess of this controversial dish.

dutch oven
Makes 3 quarts/6 to 8 moderate servings

2 TABLESPOONS EXTRA-VIRGIN OLIVE OIL
ABOUT 1 TABLESPOON UNSALTED BUTTER
3 YELLOW ONIONS, SLICED
¼ CUP ALL-PURPOSE FLOUR
¼ TEASPOON SALT
¼ TEASPOON PEPPER
3 POUNDS CUT-UP CHICKEN
3½ CUPS HOMEMADE CHICKEN STOCK OR CANNED BROTH,
   HEATED UNTIL HOT
1 TABLESPOON CHOPPED FRESH PARSLEY
1 TEASPOON CHOPPED FRESH THYME, OR ½ TEASPOON DRIED
1 TEASPOON WORCESTERSHIRE SAUCE
1 TEASPOON SUGAR
4 OUNCES LEAN COOKED HAM, CUBED
2 MEDIUM RUSSET OR WHITE POTATOES, PEELED AND DICED
1 TOMATO, PEELED, SEEDED AND CHOPPED
1 CUP FRESH OR FROZEN BABY LIMA BEANS
1 CUP FRESH OR FROZEN CORN KERNELS
SALT AND PEPPER, TO TASTE

1. Preheat the oven to 350°F. Over medium heat, heat the oil and 1 tablespoon of the butter in the dutch oven or any large stovetop-to-oven casserole. Add the onions and cook, stirring now and then, until tender, 5 to 7 minutes. Remove with a slotted spoon.

2. Combine the flour, salt and pepper in a bowl or plastic sack. Coat the chicken with the flour mixture. Brown the chicken in the dutch oven, adding butter, 1 tablespoon at a time, if needed. Remove the chicken as it browns.

3. Sprinkle any remaining flour mixture into the dutch oven and stir in the hot stock. Stir in the parsley, thyme, Worcestershire, sugar, ham, potatoes, tomato, lima beans and corn. Return the onions and meat to the

pot and stir to make sure the meat pieces are coated with the sauce. Cover the dutch oven and bake for 1 hour, or until the meat is tender.

4. Taste before serving and add salt and pepper, if needed.

Chicken Stew with Peas and Mushrooms

Grandmother started her old-fashioned chicken stew with a whole hen. Try this modern version, made easy with boneless, skinless chicken breasts.

3-quart saucepan
Makes 1 1/2 quarts/4 moderate servings

2 TABLESPOONS EXTRA-VIRGIN OLIVE OIL

1 YELLOW ONION, CHOPPED

2 SKINNY CARROTS, SLICED

1 CELERY RIB, DICED

2 TABLESPOONS UNSALTED BUTTER

8 OUNCES BUTTON MUSHROOMS, SLICED

1/4 CUP ALL-PURPOSE FLOUR

2 CUPS HOMEMADE CHICKEN STOCK OR CANNED BROTH, HEATED UNTIL HOT

1 POUND SKINLESS, BONELESS CHICKEN BREASTS, CUT INTO BITE-SIZE PIECES

1 1/2 CUPS FRESH OR FROZEN GREEN PEAS

1 TABLESPOON CHOPPED FRESH PARSLEY

1 TEASPOON CHOPPED FRESH LEMON THYME, IF AVAILABLE

1/2 TEASPOON FRESH LEMON JUICE

SALT AND PEPPER, TO TASTE

COOKED BROWN RICE, FOR SERVING

1. Heat the oil in the saucepan over medium heat. Add the onion, carrots and celery and cook, stirring often, until the onion is tender, 5 to 7 minutes. Remove with a slotted spoon and reserve.

2. Melt the butter in the pan. Add the mushrooms and cook, stirring, until tender, 5 to 7 minutes. Return the reserved vegetables to the pot; stir in the flour. Stir in the hot stock. Add the chicken, peas, parsley, thyme and lemon juice. Cover and simmer for 30 minutes, stirring now and then.

3. Add salt and pepper to taste. Serve over the hot rice.

Chicken Stew with Butter–Biscuit Dumplings

We don't have this very often. When we do, I wonder why we waited so long.

5-quart stockpot
Makes 2 quarts/5 moderate servings

2 TABLESPOONS EXTRA-VIRGIN OLIVE OIL
1 YELLOW ONION, CHOPPED
1 CARROT, DICED
1 CELERY RIB, DICED
1 FRYING CHICKEN (ABOUT 3 POUNDS), CUT UP
1 QUART HOMEMADE CHICKEN STOCK OR CANNED BROTH, HEATED
  UNTIL HOT
1 BAY LEAF
1 TEASPOON CHOPPED FRESH MARJORAM, OR ½ TEASPOON DRIED
SALT AND PEPPER, TO TASTE
BUTTER-BISCUIT DUMPLINGS (RECIPE FOLLOWS)

1. Heat 1 tablespoon of the oil in the stockpot over medium heat. Add the onion, carrot and celery and cook, stirring often, until the onion is tender, 5 to 7 minutes. Remove with a slotted spoon and reserve.

2. Add the remaining 1 tablespoon oil to the pot. Cook the chicken pieces in the oil, one layer at a time, turning once, until golden. Remove the browned pieces and reserve.

3. Pour in the stock and stir, scraping up any brown bits that stick to the bottom of the pot. Stir in the bay leaf, marjoram and reserved onion, carrots, celery and chicken. Cover and simmer for 30 to 45 minutes, or until the chicken is tender.

4. Remove the bay leaf. Skim off any fat. Add salt and pepper to taste. Remove the chicken pieces to a dish and keep warm in a low oven. (If made ahead, reheat and then remove the chicken before proceeding to the next step.)

5. Make the Butter-Biscuit Dumplings. Drop the dumplings, one at a time, onto the simmering stock. Do not crowd. Cover and simmer for 8 minutes, or until cooked all the way through.

6. Serve at once in flat soup plates, dividing the dumplings and chicken pieces among the 5 servings. Spoon the vegetable-studded gravy over all.

Butter-Biscuit Dumplings

These are not dry like some dumplings; in fact, the old-fashioned name for them is "slickers." If you just want biscuits without the stew, the dough can be cut as directed below and baked in a preheated 450°F oven for 8 minutes to make tender little butter biscuits.

Makes 36 dumplings or biscuits

1 CUP UNBLEACHED ALL-PURPOSE FLOUR
1½ TEASPOONS BAKING POWDER
¼ TEASPOON SALT
3 TABLESPOONS UNSALTED BUTTER
⅓ CUP PLUS 1 TABLESPOON SKIM MILK

1. In a mixing bowl, stir together the flour, baking powder and salt. Cut the butter into the flour mixture with a pastry blender or 2 knives. Add the milk and stir with a fork until the dry ingredients are just moistened. Turn out onto a lightly floured surface.

2. Pat or roll out the dough to a 6-inch square, about ½ inch thick. Cut into 1-inch squares. Cook the dumplings as directed in the preceding recipe.

Chunky Chowders

Thick and delicious

Traditional chowders contain three primary ingredients: salt pork, fried crisp; onions, cooked in the rendered fat; and potatoes, cubed and cooked to add body. To these are added seafood or vegetables that define the outcome. There are no strict rules, however. Milk or cream are typical ingredients, but do not appear in Manhattan-style Red Clam Chowder. Bacon can substitute for salt pork. And crackers can thicken a chowder as well as potatoes. I have gathered here favorites that I feel exhibit an agreeable chowder character.

Country Corn Chowder

In the summer when the sweet corn is ripening, I process several dozen ears at a time, making fresh cream-style corn to pack in the freezer. As I am cutting the corn from the ears, at least 2 cups of it gets set aside for making a small batch of this soup. When cooked until the corn is just done and no longer, it has the fresh taste of corn on the cob. It's perfect with a sliced tomato and cucumber salad.

3-quart saucepan
Makes 5 cups/4 moderate servings

3 SLICES LEAN BACON, DICED
1 YELLOW ONION, CHOPPED
¼ CUP FINELY CHOPPED GREEN BELL PEPPER
KERNELS AND SCRAPINGS FROM 4 EARS OF FRESH SWEET CORN
   (ABOUT 2 CUPS)
1 CUP HOMEMADE CHICKEN STOCK OR CANNED BROTH
2 CUPS SKIM MILK OR LIGHT CREAM
6 SALTINE CRACKERS, CRUSHED
SALT AND WHITE PEPPER, TO TASTE
1 CUP (4 OUNCES) SHREDDED LOWFAT CHEDDAR CHEESE

1. In the saucepan, sauté the bacon over medium heat until cooked through and almost crisp. Spoon off any rendered fat.

2. Add the onion and bell pepper to the pot and cook, stirring, until the vegetables are limp and partially cooked, about 2 minutes. Stir in the corn and stock. Increase the heat and bring the mixture to a boil. Reduce the heat to a simmer and cook, stirring occasionally, until the corn just tests done, 2 or 3 minutes. Test by tasting a kernel; do not overcook.

3. Stir in the milk and crushed crackers. Cook, stirring, until the crackers thicken the soup, 2 to 3 minutes. Add salt and pepper to taste. Add the cheese and stir gently to melt. Serve in pottery bowls.

Deutsch Ham Chowder

This hearty soup has a mild sweet-sour flavor—perfect with slices of pumpernickel rye bread and a mixed dried fruit compote.

5-quart stockpot
Makes 3 quarts/6 generous servings

2 TABLESPOONS EXTRA-VIRGIN OLIVE OIL

4 YELLOW ONIONS, FINELY CHOPPED

2 TABLESPOONS BROWN SUGAR

2 TABLESPOONS CIDER VINEGAR

3 CUPS CUBED BAKED HAM ($\frac{1}{4}$-INCH CUBES)

6 CUPS FINELY CHOPPED CABBAGE (ABOUT 12 OUNCES)

4 MEDIUM RUSSET OR WHITE POTATOES, PEELED AND CUT INTO $\frac{1}{4}$-INCH CUBES

2 QUARTS HOMEMADE CHICKEN STOCK OR CANNED BROTH, HEATED UNTIL HOT

SALT AND PEPPER, TO TASTE

3 TABLESPOONS UNSALTED BUTTER

3 TABLESPOONS ALL-PURPOSE FLOUR

$\frac{1}{2}$ TEASPOON CHOPPED CARAWAY SEEDS

1. Warm the oil in the stockpot over medium-high heat. Add the onions and cook, stirring constantly, until tender, 2 to 3 minutes. Remove the pot from the heat. Stir in the sugar and vinegar. Let stand for 5 minutes to marinate the onions.

2. Stir the ham, cabbage and potatoes into the onion mixture. Add the hot stock, cover and simmer until the potatoes are tender, about 30 minutes.

3. Taste the soup and add salt and pepper, if needed. Knead together the butter, flour and caraway seeds. Uncover the soup. Drop the butter mixture into the soup, bit by bit, stirring constantly. Continue to cook, stirring, until the soup thickens. Serve in heavy pottery bowls.

Bean and Bacon Chowder

Navy beans and potatoes make a good combination in a chowder. Serve with Brown Bread Muffins (page 207).

105

3-quart saucepan
Makes 1½ quarts/4 moderate servings

4 OUNCES THICK-SLICED BACON, DICED
1 YELLOW ONION, CHOPPED
2 CELERY RIBS WITH LEAVES, CHOPPED
2 MEDIUM RUSSET OR WHITE POTATOES, PEELED AND DICED
1 BAY LEAF
2 CUPS HOME-COOKED OR CANNED NAVY BEANS
1½ CUPS SKIM MILK OR LIGHT CREAM
SALT AND PEPPER, TO TASTE
CHOPPED FRESH PARSLEY, FOR GARNISH

1. Sauté the bacon in the saucepan until cooked through and almost crisp. Spoon off all but 1 tablespoon of the rendered fat. Add the onion and the celery and cook over medium heat with the lid slightly ajar, stirring often, until the onion is tender, 5 to 7 minutes.

2. Add the potatoes, bay leaf and 1½ cups of water. Cover and simmer until the potatoes are tender, 30 to 45 minutes.

3. Remove the bay leaf. Mash the beans with a potato masher or fork and add to the pot along with the milk. Heat thoroughly but do not boil.

4. Add salt and pepper to taste. Serve in heavy bowls. Sprinkle some parsley over each serving.

Cheeseburger Chowder

This is a good family pleaser. As with many soups, it is even better the second day. If you wish to make it ahead, wait until reheating to add the cheese.

3-quart saucepan
Makes 2 quarts/4 hearty servings

2 TABLESPOONS EXTRA-VIRGIN OLIVE OIL

1 YELLOW ONION, CHOPPED

3 CELERY RIBS WITH LEAVES, CHOPPED

1/2 GREEN BELL PEPPER, SEEDED AND DICED

2 TABLESPOONS CHOPPED FRESH PARSLEY

1 POUND LEAN GROUND BEEF

2 MEDIUM RUSSET OR WHITE POTATOES, PEELED AND DICED

1 TEASPOON WORCESTERSHIRE SAUCE

2 CUPS HOMEMADE BEEF STOCK OR CANNED BROTH

1 1/2 TABLESPOONS CORNSTARCH

2 CUPS SKIM MILK OR LIGHT CREAM

1 CUP (4 OUNCES) SHREDDED SHARP CHEDDAR CHEESE

SALT AND PEPPER, TO TASTE

CHOPPED DILL PICKLES, FOR GARNISH

1. Warm the olive oil in the saucepan. Add the onion, celery, bell pepper and parsley and cook over medium heat, with the lid slightly ajar, stirring occasionally, until the onion is tender, 5 to 7 minutes.

2. Uncover the pot. Add the beef and brown over medium-high heat. Add the potatoes, Worcestershire and stock. Cover and simmer, until the potatoes are tender, about 45 minutes.

3. Stir the cornstarch into the milk and add to the pot. Simmer, uncovered, stirring constantly, until thickened, about 3 minutes. Add the cheese and simmer, stirring gently, just until melted.

4. Add salt and pepper, if needed. Serve in heavy pottery bowls. Garnish with the chopped pickles.

White Clam Chowder

This is a New England-style chowder—with cream and no tomatoes. The Manhattan style, with tomatoes and no cream, is next. Three cans (6 1/2 ounces each) of chopped or minced clams can be substituted for the fresh in either recipe.

5-quart nonreactive stockpot and 3-quart nonreactive saucepan
Makes 1½ quarts/4 moderate servings

½ CUP DRY WHITE WINE
3 DOZEN CHOWDER CLAMS, SCRUBBED WELL
¼ CUP DICED SALT PORK
1 YELLOW ONION, FINELY CHOPPED
3 SCALLIONS WITH SOME OF THE GREEN TOPS, THINLY SLICED
1 GARLIC CLOVE, MINCED
3 MEDIUM RUSSET OR WHITE POTATOES, PEELED AND DICED
½ TEASPOON CHOPPED FRESH THYME, OR ¼ TEASPOON DRIED
1 BAY LEAF
1 WHOLE ALLSPICE BERRY
2 CUPS LIGHT CREAM
6 SALTINE CRACKERS, CRUSHED
SALT AND PEPPER, TO TASTE
THINLY-SLICED SCALLIONS, FOR GARNISH

1. In the stockpot, bring the wine and ½ cup of water to a simmer. Add the clams, cover and simmer for 4 minutes. Remove the opened clams. Steam the remaining clams for 4 minutes. Discard any that do not open.

2. Remove the clams from their shells and reserve their liquor. Strain the liquor through a sieve lined with dampened cheesecloth into a bowl. Coarsely chop the clams and combine with the liquor; reserve.

3. Sauté the salt pork in the saucepan over medium heat until the fat is rendered and the pork is nicely browned. Add the onion, scallions and garlic and sauté until the vegetables are golden, 7 to 10 minutes.

4. Add the potatoes, thyme, bay leaf, allspice and 1 cup of water. Cover and cook until the potatoes are tender, about 30 minutes.

5. Remove the bay leaf and allspice. Stir in the cream and crushed crackers. Simmer gently, stirring often, just until thickened.

6. Add the clams and their liquor and bring to a simmer. Cook for 2 to 3 minutes, but do not boil. Taste and add salt and pepper, if needed. Garnish each serving with the scallions.

Red Clam Chowder

This is the chowder with tomatoes—Manhattan-style—considered a blasphemy by some New Englanders.

5-quart nonreactive stockpot and 3-quart nonreactive saucepan
Makes 2 quarts/4 hearty servings

$\frac{1}{2}$ CUP DRY WHITE WINE

3 DOZEN CHOWDER CLAMS, SCRUBBED WELL

$\frac{1}{4}$ CUP DICED SALT PORK

1 YELLOW ONION, CHOPPED

1 GREEN BELL PEPPER, SEEDED AND DICED

2 CARROTS, CHOPPED

2 CELERY RIBS, CHOPPED

1 TABLESPOON CHOPPED FRESH PARSLEY

$\frac{1}{2}$ TEASPOON CHOPPED FRESH THYME, OR $\frac{1}{4}$ TEASPOON DRIED

1 BAY LEAF

2 CUPS FRESH OR CANNED CHOPPED TOMATOES

3 MEDIUM RUSSET OR WHITE POTATOES, PEELED AND DICED

SALT AND PEPPER, TO TASTE

CHOPPED FRESH PARSLEY, FOR SERVING

1. In the stockpot, bring the wine and $\frac{1}{2}$ cup of water to a simmer. Add the clams, cover and simmer for 4 minutes. Remove the opened clams. Steam the remaining clams for 4 minutes. Discard any that do not open.

2. Remove the clams from their shells and reserve their liquor. Strain the liquor through a sieve lined with dampened cheesecloth into a bowl. Coarsely chop the clams and combine with the liquor; reserve.

3. Sauté the salt pork in the saucepan over medium heat until the fat is rendered and the pork is nicely browned. Add the onion, bell pepper, carrots, celery and parsley. Cook, partially covered, stirring often, until the vegetables are crisp-tender, 5 to 7 minutes.

4. Stir in the thyme, bay leaf, tomatoes, potatoes and 2 cups of water. Cover and cook until the potatoes are tender, about 30 minutes.

5. Remove the bay leaf. Add the clams and their liquor and bring to a simmer. Cook for 2 to 3 minutes. Taste and add salt and pepper, if needed. Serve in flat soup plates. Sprinkle each serving with the parsley.

Salmon Chowder

This is easy and delicious. Serve with a pineapple-cabbage slaw and toasted buttered crackers. You can substitute one can (15 ounces) red salmon for the fresh, if you wish.

3-quart saucepan
Makes 2 quarts/4 hearty servings

3 SLICES LEAN BACON, DICED
6 SCALLIONS WITH SOME OF THE GREEN TOPS, SLICED
½ GREEN BELL PEPPER, SEEDED AND DICED
3 MEDIUM RUSSET OR WHITE POTATOES, PEELED AND DICED
¼ CUP MINCED FRESH PARSLEY
1 TEASPOON MINCED FRESH DILL, OR ¼ TEASPOON DRIED
1 POUND FRESH SALMON, CUT INTO 1-INCH CHUNKS
3 CUPS SKIM MILK OR LIGHT CREAM
6 SALTINE CRACKERS, CRUSHED
SALT AND PEPPER, TO TASTE

1. Sauté the bacon in the saucepan until crisp. Remove with a slotted spoon and drain. Spoon out all but 1 tablespoon of the rendered fat.

2. Add the scallions and bell pepper to the pan and cook over medium heat with the lid slightly ajar, stirring often, until the vegetables are tender, 5 to 7 minutes.

3. Stir in the potatoes, parsley, dill, reserved bacon and 2 cups of water. Simmer, covered, until the potatoes are tender, 30 to 45 minutes.

4. Stir in the salmon, milk and crackers. Simmer, stirring often, for about 15 minutes, or until the fish flakes and the soup thickens. Taste, adding salt and pepper if needed.

Tuna Chowder

This is an easy-to-make family-style soup with two variations.

3-quart saucepan
Makes 1½ quarts/4 moderate servings

2 TABLESPOONS EXTRA-VIRGIN OLIVE OIL
2 TABLESPOONS UNSALTED BUTTER
1 CARROT, FINELY CHOPPED
1 CELERY RIB, FINELY CHOPPED
1 YELLOW ONION, FINELY CHOPPED
¼ CUP ALL-PURPOSE FLOUR
2 CUPS SKIM MILK OR LIGHT CREAM
2 CUPS HOMEMADE CHICKEN STOCK OR CANNED BROTH
1 BAY LEAF
1 TABLESPOON CHOPPED FRESH PARSLEY
2 CANS (6¼ OUNCES EACH) WATER-PACKED CHUNK LIGHT TUNA, DRAINED
SALT AND PEPPER, TO TASTE
CHOPPED FRESH CHIVES, FOR GARNISH

1. Heat the oil and butter in the saucepan over medium heat. Add the carrot, celery and onion and sauté until the vegetables are crisp-tender, 7 to 10 minutes.

2. Stir in the flour. Add the milk and stock and stir well. Add the bay leaf and parsley. Cook, stirring often, until thick and bubbly.

3. Stir in the tuna. Taste and add salt and pepper, if needed. Remove the bay leaf. Garnish each serving with the chopped chives.

Tuna–Cheese Chowder

Substitute 1 cup (4 ounces) shredded cheddar cheese for 1 can of the tuna in Tuna Chowder. Proceed as before.

Corn and Tuna Chowder

Substitute 1 cup cooked canned or frozen whole kernel corn for 1 can of the tuna in Tuna Chowder. Proceed as before.

Succotash Chowder

This is an all-vegetable chowder using the succotash combination—lima beans and corn. If your schedule permits, make it a day ahead because it's even better the second day. Good with Whole-Grain French Bread (page 194).

3-quart saucepan
Makes 2 quarts/6 moderate servings

1 YELLOW ONION, FINELY CHOPPED
2 MEDIUM RUSSET OR WHITE POTATOES, PEELED AND DICED
2 CUPS FRESH OR FROZEN BABY LIMA BEANS
2 CUPS FRESH OR FROZEN CORN KERNELS
1/2 TEASPOON CHOPPED FRESH ROSEMARY, OR 1/4 TEASPOON DRIED
1/2 TEASPOON CHOPPED FRESH THYME, OR 1/4 TEASPOON DRIED
1/2 TEASPOON CHOPPED FRESH SAGE, OR 1/4 TEASPOON DRIED
2 CUPS SKIM MILK OR LIGHT CREAM
4 TABLESPOONS UNSALTED BUTTER
1/4 CUP ALL–PURPOSE FLOUR

SALT AND WHITE PEPPER, TO TASTE

CRISP-FRIED CRUMBLED BACON OR CHOPPED FRESH PARSLEY, FOR
GARNISH

1. Bring 4 cups of water to a boil in the saucepan. Add the onion, potatoes, lima beans, corn, rosemary, thyme and sage. Simmer, covered, for 1 hour.

2. Stir in the milk and bring to a gentle simmer.

3. Knead the butter and flour together and stir into the soup, bit by bit. Cook, stirring, until thickened. Add salt and pepper, if desired. Garnish the servings with bacon or parsley.

Parsnip Chowder

If you like the sweet flavor of parsnips, you will want to try this old-fashioned chowder.

3-quart saucepan
Makes 1 1/2 quarts/4 moderate servings

3 SLICES LEAN BACON, DICED

1 YELLOW ONION, CHOPPED

1 POUND TENDER YOUNG PARSNIPS, PEELED AND CHOPPED

2 MEDIUM RUSSET OR WHITE POTATOES, PEELED AND DICED

1/4 CUP CHOPPED FRESH PARSLEY

2 CUPS HOMEMADE CHICKEN STOCK OR CANNED BROTH

1 1/2 TABLESPOONS CORNSTARCH

2 CUPS SKIM MILK OR LIGHT CREAM

SALT AND WHITE PEPPER, TO TASTE

CHOPPED FRESH PARSLEY, FOR GARNISH

1. Sauté the bacon in the saucepan until crisp. Remove with a slotted spoon. Spoon off all but 1 tablespoon of the rendered fat.

2. Add the onion and cook, partially covered, stirring often, until tender, 5 to 7 minutes.

3. Stir in the parsnips, potatoes, parsley, reserved bacon and stock. Simmer, covered, until the vegetables are tender, 30 to 45 minutes.

4. Stir the cornstarch into the milk and add to the pot. Cook, stirring, until the soup thickens, about 3 minutes. Taste and add salt and pepper, if needed. Serve in flat soup plates. Garnish with the fresh parsley.

Broccoli-Cauliflower Chowder

This calls for equal amounts of cauliflower and broccoli, but it can be made with a double quantity of either ingredient or the "new" vegetable, brocco-flower.

3-quart saucepan
Makes 2 quarts/4 moderate servings

1 QUART HOMEMADE CHICKEN STOCK OR CANNED BROTH
1 MEDIUM RUSSET OR WHITE POTATO, PEELED AND DICED
1 YELLOW ONION, CHOPPED
1 CARROT, FINELY CHOPPED
1 CELERY RIB, FINELY CHOPPED
1 TABLESPOON CHOPPED FRESH PARSLEY
1/2 TEASPOON CHOPPED FRESH DILL, OR 1/4 TEASPOON DRIED
2 CUPS SMALL CAULIFLOWER FLORETS
2 CUPS SMALL BROCCOLI FLORETS
2 CUPS SKIM MILK OR LIGHT CREAM
2 TABLESPOONS ALL-PURPOSE FLOUR
2 TABLESPOONS UNSALTED BUTTER
1 SMALL PACKAGE (3 OUNCES) CREAM CHEESE, CUT INTO CHUNKS
SALT AND WHITE PEPPER, TO TASTE
FRESHLY GRATED NUTMEG, FOR SERVING

1. Combine the stock, potato, onion, carrot, celery, parsley and dill in the saucepan. Simmer, covered, until the vegetables are tender, about 30 minutes.

2. Stir in the cauliflower and broccoli and cook just until crisp-tender, about 10 minutes.

3. Add the milk and bring just to a simmer. Meanwhile, knead the flour and the butter together. Add it, bit by bit, to the chowder, stirring all the while. Drop in the cream cheese, piece by piece, and stir until the cheese melts.

4. Taste and add salt and pepper, if needed. Serve in white bowls, if you have them. Top each serving with a dusting of freshly grated nutmeg.

Potato Chowder

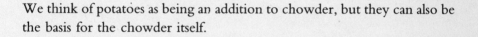

We think of potatoes as being an addition to chowder, but they can also be the basis for the chowder itself.

3-quart saucepan
Makes 2 quarts/6 moderate servings

1 QUART HOMEMADE FISH OR CHICKEN STOCK OR CANNED BROTH
6 MEDIUM RUSSET OR WHITE POTATOES, PEELED AND DICED
2 YELLOW ONIONS, CHOPPED
1 CARROT, CHOPPED
1 CELERY RIB, CHOPPED
1 TABLESPOON CHOPPED FRESH PARSLEY
½ TEASPOON CHOPPED FRESH THYME, OR ¼ TEASPOON DRIED
½ TEASPOON CHOPPED FRESH DILL, OR ¼ TEASPOON DRIED
1 BAY LEAF
ABOUT 1 CUP SKIM MILK OR LIGHT CREAM
CHOPPED FRESH PARSLEY, FOR GARNISH

1. Combine the stock, potatoes, onions, carrot, celery, parsley, thyme, dill and bay leaf in the saucepan. Simmer, covered, for 1 hour.

2. Remove the bay leaf. Stir in the milk to thin the chowder—the amount will vary according to how much the potatoes break up while cooking. Serve in heavy pottery bowls, garnished with the parsley.

Peppery Chilis

To bring a glint to your eye (or is that a tear?)

There is nothing better for warming up a blustery winter day than a steaming bowl of chili. A few of my chilis are all-meat, but I often use beans of one or more types and sometimes grains. Some chili-heads say you should never adulterate chili with beans, but I relish their flavor and appreciate the added fiber.

You are not seeing typos in the text of this chapter. "Chili" is considered correct for a bowl of the brew; "chile" is used when referring to a chile pepper; and "chili powder" is the proper spelling for a blend of ground chiles and herbs, such as cumin and oregano.

The recipes list the option of using store-bought, pre-mixed chili powder or pure ground chiles. The chili powder will give your chilis the safety of a middle-of-the-road flavor. The ground chiles will produce authentic Southwestern seasonings that vary in intensity from mild to hot—it's fun to experiment. Find them in specialty food shops or order by mail from: The Chile Shop, 109 East Water Street, Santa Fe, NM 87501; (505) 983-6080.

Green Tomato Chili

When cold weather threatens your garden, bring in the green tomatoes before they get frostbitten. Use some in this easy-to-make chili. It's great for lunch on a crisp fall day.

3-quart nonreactive saucepan
Makes 1 1/2 quarts/4 moderate servings

2 TABLESPOONS EXTRA-VIRGIN OLIVE OIL
2 GARLIC CLOVES, MINCED
2 YELLOW ONIONS, CHOPPED
1 POUND LEAN BEEF ROUND OR BOTTOM ROUND, COARSELY
   CHOPPED
2 CUPS PEELED, CHOPPED GREEN TOMATOES
GRATED ZEST OF 1 LEMON
1 TABLESPOON FRESH LEMON JUICE
2 CUPS HOME-COOKED OR CANNED RED KIDNEY BEANS
2 TEASPOONS CHILI POWDER OR PURE GROUND CHILES
1/8 TEASPOON GROUND CAYENNE PEPPER
1 TABLESPOON STONE-GROUND CORNMEAL
SALT AND PEPPER, TO TASTE

1. Heat the oil in the saucepan over medium heat. Add the garlic and onions and sauté until the onion is tender, 5 to 7 minutes.

2. Add the beef and cook, stirring, until it loses its red color.

3. Stir in the tomatoes, lemon zest, lemon juice, kidney beans and 2 cups of water.

4. Combine the chili powder, cayenne and cornmeal. Stir the spice mixture into the chili. Bring to a gentle boil, stirring all the while. Reduce the heat to a simmer and cook for 1 to 2 hours, stirring occasionally, until the mixture thickens. This chili can be cooked covered or uncovered. Uncovered, it will thicken more quickly.

5. Taste and add salt and pepper, if needed. Serve in heavy pottery bowls.

Wheat Berry Chili

The complementary proteins of wheat berries and pinto beans make a great nutrition combination for a meatless chili that's loaded with flavor and fiber. Good with a simple green salad and hot corn bread.

3-quart saucepan and a nonstick skillet
Makes 5 cups/4 moderate servings

1 CUP DRIED PINTO BEANS, RINSED AND DRAINED
1 CUP WHEAT BERRIES
1/2 BAY LEAF
1 TEASPOON EXTRA-VIRGIN OLIVE OIL
2 GARLIC CLOVES, MINCED
1 YELLOW ONION, CHOPPED
1 TEASPOON GROUND CUMIN
1 TABLESPOON CHILI POWDER OR PURE GROUND CHILES
1 TABLESPOON STONE-GROUND CORNMEAL
SALT AND PEPPER, TO TASTE
SHREDDED LOWFAT CHEDDAR CHEESE, FOR GARNISH

1. In the saucepan, combine the pinto beans and wheat berries. Add 2 quarts of water and the bay leaf. Bring to a boil, uncovered. Reduce the heat to a simmer, cover and cook for 1 hour.

2. In the nonstick skillet, heat the oil over medium heat. Add the garlic and onion and sauté until the onion is tender. Add to the pot.

3. Stir together the cumin, chili powder and cornmeal; stir into the pot. Cook at a simmer, uncovered, stirring occasionally, until the beans and the wheat berries are tender, and the chili is thick, 3 hours or longer. Add water to the pot if the chili dries out during cooking.

4. Remove the bay leaf. Add salt and pepper, if desired. Serve in heavy pottery bowls. Pass the shredded cheese at the table.

Mixed Bean Chili with Vegetables

The combination of beans used here is one that pleases me, but it can be varied. Use the dibs and dabs of whatever dried beans you have leftover from other recipes, measuring 1½ cups in all.

5-quart nonreactive stockpot
Makes 2½ quarts/8 moderate servings

½ CUP DRIED KIDNEY BEANS, RINSED AND DRAINED

½ CUP DRIED BABY LIMA BEANS, RINSED AND DRAINED

½ CUP DRIED BLACK OR TURTLE BEANS, RINSED AND DRAINED

1 TABLESPOON CANOLA OIL

2 YELLOW ONIONS, CHOPPED

2 GARLIC CLOVES, MINCED

2 CELERY RIBS WITH LEAVES, CHOPPED

2 CARROTS, CHOPPED

½ GREEN BELL PEPPER, SEEDED AND DICED

1 BAY LEAF

1 CAN (8 OUNCES) TOMATO SAUCE

2 TOMATOES, PEELED, SEEDED AND CHOPPED

¼ CUP CHOPPED FRESH PARSLEY

1 TABLESPOON STONE-GROUND CORNMEAL

1½ TABLESPOONS CHILI POWDER OR PURE GROUND CHILES

1 TEASPOON GROUND OREGANO

1 TEASPOON GROUND CUMIN

¼ TEASPOON GROUND ALLSPICE

SALT AND PEPPER, TO TASTE

1. Combine all of the beans with 4½ cups of water and soak for 6 to 8 hours or overnight. Alternately, bring the water to a boil, add the beans, and boil for 2 minutes. Remove from the heat, cover and let stand for 1 hour. Drain

2. Heat the oil in the stockpot over medium heat. Add the onions,

garlic, celery, carrots and bell pepper. Cook, stirring often, until the onion is tender, 5 to 7 minutes.

    3. Add the beans, bay leaf and 4½ cups of water. Bring to a boil. Reduce the heat to a simmer, cover and cook for 2 hours, or until the beans are tender.

    4. Remove the bay leaf. Add the tomato sauce, tomatoes and parsley. Stir together the cornmeal, chili powder, oregano, cumin and allspice. Stir the spices into the pot. Simmer, uncovered, stirring now and then, for 15 minutes. Add water if the chili gets too thick.

    5. Taste and add salt and pepper, if needed. Serve in heavy pottery bowls.

White Chili

If you don't eat anything that doesn't swim or fly, here's the chili for you. Ground chicken or turkey is used instead of beef or pork. Corn replaces the usual beans.

3-quart saucepan
Makes 1¼ quarts/3 moderate servings

1 TABLESPOON EXTRA-VIRGIN OLIVE OIL

1 YELLOW ONION, FINELY CHOPPED

1 GARLIC CLOVE, MINCED

2 TABLESPOONS FINELY DICED GREEN BELL PEPPER

1 POUND GROUND CHICKEN OR TURKEY

2 TABLESPOONS ALL-PURPOSE FLOUR

1 TEASPOON CORNMEAL

1 TABLESPOON CHILI POWDER OR PURE GROUND CHILES

½ TEASPOON GROUND OREGANO

½ TEASPOON GROUND CUMIN

2 CUPS HOMEMADE CHICKEN STOCK OR CANNED BROTH, HEATED
UNTIL HOT

2 TABLESPOONS CANNED CHOPPED GREEN CHILES (OPTIONAL)

1 CAN (12 OUNCES) WHITE WHOLE KERNEL CORN, DRAINED

1. Heat the oil in the saucepan over medium heat. Add the onion, garlic and bell pepper and cook, stirring constantly, until the onion is tender, 5 to 7 minutes.

2. Add the chicken and cook until opaque. Remove the pan from the heat.

3. Stir together the flour, cornmeal, chili powder, oregano and cumin. Sprinkle the mixture over the chicken. Stir in the hot stock.

4. Return the pan to medium heat. Add the chiles and corn. Reduce the heat to a simmer and cook, uncovered, stirring often, for 15 minutes. Serve in ceramic bowls.

Black Bean Chili

This chili makes a deep brown gravy. Be sure to offer bread for soaking up every bit.

5-quart nonreactive stockpot
Makes 2³/₄ quarts/8 moderate servings

2 TABLESPOONS CANOLA OIL
1 POUND LEAN BEEF, COARSELY CHOPPED
1 POUND LEAN PORK, COARSELY CHOPPED
1 YELLOW ONION, FINELY CHOPPED
2 GARLIC CLOVES, MINCED
2 CUPS HOMEMADE HAM STOCK, BEEF STOCK OR CANNED BROTH
2 CUPS FRESH OR CANNED CHOPPED TOMATOES
1 TABLESPOON FRESH LEMON JUICE
1 CAN (4 OUNCES) ROASTED, PEELED AND DICED GREEN CHILES
4 CUPS HOME-COOKED OR CANNED BLACK OR TURTLE BEANS
1 TABLESPOON ALL-PURPOSE FLOUR
1 TABLESPOON STONE-GROUND CORNMEAL
2 TABLESPOONS CHILI POWDER OR PURE GROUND CHILES
1 TABLESPOON PAPRIKA
¹/₈ TEASPOON CAYENNE PEPPER
SALT AND PEPPER, TO TASTE
FRESH LEMON WEDGES, FOR SERVING
CHOPPED SCALLIONS, FOR SERVING

1. Heat the oil in the stockpot over medium-high heat. Add the beef, pork, onion and garlic and cook, stirring often, until the meats are browned, about 5 minutes.

2. Stir in the stock, tomatoes, lemon juice and chiles. Simmer, covered, for 1 hour.

3. Uncover and add the beans. Stir together the flour, cornmeal, chili powder, paprika and cayenne. Stir the mixture into the meats. Simmer, uncovered, stirring often, for 15 minutes. Add a small amount of water if the chili gets too thick.

4. Add salt and pepper to taste. Serve in flat soup plates. Place a wedge of lemon on the side of each plate. Pass the scallions at the table.

Chocolate Chili

No, this isn't a result of going too long without chocolate chip cookies. Chili can be made with chocolate to create a Mexican *mole*-like flavor. In this recipe, I have used unsweetened cocoa to provide the flavor without the fat.

5-quart nonreactive stockpot or dutch oven
Makes 2 1/2 quarts/8 moderate servings

3 TABLESPOONS CANOLA OIL
1 POUND LEAN BEEF ROUND OR BOTTOM ROUND, CUT IN 1/4-INCH CUBES
1 POUND LEAN PORK LOIN, CUT IN 1/4-INCH CUBES
2 LARGE YELLOW ONIONS, COARSELY CHOPPED
3 GARLIC CLOVES, MINCED
4 CUPS HOME-COOKED OR CANNED RED KIDNEY BEANS
1 CAN (8 OUNCES) TOMATO SAUCE
1/4 TEASPOON CRUSHED RED PEPPER FLAKES
1 BAY LEAF
1 TABLESPOON MASA HARINA OR STONE-GROUND CORNMEAL
2 TABLESPOONS CHILI POWDER OR PURE GROUND CHILES
2 TABLESPOONS UNSWEETENED COCOA POWDER
2 TEASPOONS GROUND CINNAMON
2 TEASPOONS SALT (OPTIONAL)

1. Heat 1 tablespoon of the oil in the stockpot over medium-high heat. Add the beef and pork and cook, stirring, until the meats are browned on all sides, about 5 minutes. Remove to a dish.

2. Add the remaining 2 tablespoons oil to the pot along with the onions and garlic. Sauté for 2 minutes. Return the meat and any accumulated juices to the pot. Stir in the beans, tomato sauce, red pepper flakes, bay leaf and 1 cup of water. Cover and simmer for 1 hour.

3. Uncover the pot. Stir together the masa harina, chili powder,

cocoa, cinnamon and salt. Stir this mixture into the chili and simmer gently, uncovered, for 45 minutes. Add a small amount of water if the chili gets too thick.

    4. Adjust the seasonings, if necessary. Serve in heavy pottery bowls.

Chili con Carne

This is quick and easy and very tasty—good with corn bread and cold milk.

3-quart nonreactive saucepan
Makes 1 1/2 quarts/4 moderate servings

2 TABLESPOONS CANOLA OIL
1 YELLOW ONION, THINLY SLICED
1/2 GREEN BELL PEPPER, SEEDED AND CHOPPED
2 GARLIC CLOVES, MINCED
1 POUND GROUND CHUCK
2 CUPS HOME-COOKED OR CANNED RED KIDNEY BEANS
2 CUPS FRESH OR CANNED CHOPPED TOMATOES
1 CAN (8 OUNCES) TOMATO SAUCE
1 TABLESPOON CHILI POWDER OR PURE GROUND CHILES
1/2 TEASPOON GROUND CUMIN
1 TEASPOON SALT (OPTIONAL)
FRESHLY GROUND PEPPER, TO TASTE

    1. Heat the oil in the saucepan over medium heat. Add the onion and bell pepper and cook, stirring often, until the onion is tender, 5 to 7 minutes.

    2. Stir in the garlic and beef and cook, stirring often, until the meat loses all pink color, about 5 minutes.

    3. Add the beans, tomatoes and tomato sauce. Stir in the chili powder, cumin and salt. Simmer, uncovered, stirring now and then, for 20 minutes. Add a small amount of water if the chili gets too thick.

4. Add freshly ground pepper to taste. Serve in heavy pottery bowls.

Ranch House Chili

This chili is thickened with wonderful gravy from the slow-cooked pinto beans, with just a touch of tomato to round out the flavor.

5-quart nonreactive stockpot or dutch oven and a large skillet
Makes 3 1/2 quarts/8 hearty servings

1 POUND DRIED PINTO BEANS, RINSED AND DRAINED
4 SLICES LEAN BACON, DICED
2 YELLOW ONIONS, COARSELY CHOPPED
1 GREEN BELL PEPPER, SEEDED AND DICED
2 1/2 POUNDS LEAN BEEF ROUND OR BOTTOM ROUND, COARSELY
   CHOPPED
1 CAN (4 OUNCES) ROASTED, PEELED AND DICED GREEN CHILES
2 TEASPOONS SALT (OPTIONAL)
1/4 TEASPOON COARSELY GROUND BLACK PEPPER
2 TABLESPOONS CHILI POWDER OR PURE GROUND CHILES
1 TEASPOON PAPRIKA
1/4 TEASPOON CRUSHED RED PEPPER FLAKES
ABOUT 2 CUPS TOMATO JUICE
CORN BREAD, FOR SERVING

1. Combine the beans and 6 cups of water and soak for 6 to 8 hours or overnight. Alternately, bring the water to a boil, add the beans, and boil for 2 minutes. Remove from heat, cover and let stand for 1 hour.

2. Drain the beans. Combine with 6 cups of fresh water and bring to a boil. Reduce the heat to a simmer, cover and cook, stirring now and then, for 2 hours, or until tender.

3. When the beans are almost done, cook the bacon in the skillet

over medium heat until crisp. Remove with a slotted spoon and add the bacon to the beans.

    4. Add the onions, bell pepper and beef to the fat in the skillet and cook, stirring often, until all pink color is gone from the beef.

    5. Remove the meat and vegetables with a slotted spoon and add to the beans. Stir in the chiles, salt, pepper, chili powder, paprika, red pepper flakes and 2 cups of the tomato juice. Simmer, uncovered, stirring now and then, for 30 minutes, or until thick. Add additional tomato juice if the chili gets too thick.

    6. Serve in glass or enameled pie plates with a slab of corn bread atop each serving.

Texas Red

With the rice and beans, this makes a hearty Southwestern-style meal. Buy a carton of fresh salsa from the dairy case to pass at the table.

5-quart nonreactive stockpot
Makes 2 1/2 quarts/10 moderate servings

3 TABLESPOONS CANOLA OIL

3 POUNDS BONELESS CHUCK, CUT INTO 1/4–INCH CUBES AND
  PATTED DRY

1 YELLOW ONION, VERY FINELY CHOPPED

2 GARLIC CLOVES, MINCED

1 TABLESPOON ALL-PURPOSE FLOUR

1 TABLESPOON STONE-GROUND CORNMEAL

2 TABLESPOONS CHILI POWDER OR PURE GROUND CHILES

1 TABLESPOON PAPRIKA

1 TEASPOON GROUND CUMIN

1/4 TEASPOON GROUND CAYENNE PEPPER

3 CUPS HOMEMADE BEEF STOCK OR CANNED BROTH

1 LARGE CAN (16 OUNCES) TOMATO SAUCE

1 CAN (6 OUNCES) TOMATO PASTE

1 BAY LEAF

SALT AND PEPPER, TO TASTE

COOKED WHITE RICE, FOR SERVING

HOME–COOKED OR CANNED PINTO BEANS, FOR SERVING

HOT PEPPER SAUCE, FOR PASSING AT THE TABLE

FRESH SALSA, FOR PASSING AT THE TABLE

1. Warm the oil in the stockpot over medium-high heat. Add the beef, onion and garlic and cook, stirring constantly, until the meat browns on all sides, about 5 minutes. Remove from the heat.

2. Stir together the flour, cornmeal, chili powder, paprika, cumin and cayenne. Stir the mixture into the meat mixture. Stir in the stock, tomato sauce, tomato paste and bay leaf. Return to low heat and simmer, covered, for 1 hour.

3. Uncover; remove the bay leaf. Simmer gently, uncovered, for 45 minutes. Add a small amount of water if the chili gets too thick.

4. Taste and add salt and pepper, if needed. Serve on rimmed plates flanked by steaming hot rice and pinto beans. Pass the hot pepper sauce and salsa.

Super Bowl Chili

Let the chili simmer while you watch the game. For a serve-yourself buffet, offer coleslaw, tortilla chips and a choice of cold milk or beer.

5-quart nonreactive stockpot or dutch oven
Makes 4 1/2 quarts/12 moderate servings

1/4 CUP CANOLA OIL

3 POUNDS LEAN BEEF ROUND OR BOTTOM ROUND, COARSELY CHOPPED

1 POUND LEAN PORK LOIN, COARSELY CHOPPED

4 LARGE YELLOW ONIONS, COARSELY CHOPPED

6 GARLIC CLOVES, MINCED

1/4 CUP PLUS 2 TABLESPOONS CHILI POWDER OR PURE GROUND CHILES

1 TABLESPOON SALT (OPTIONAL)

1 TABLESPOON GROUND CUMIN

1 TABLESPOON GROUND OREGANO

2 CUPS HOMEMADE BEEF STOCK OR CANNED BROTH

1 CAN (12 OUNCES) BEER

1 LARGE CAN (16 OUNCES) TOMATO SAUCE

4 CUPS FRESH OR CANNED CHOPPED TOMATOES

6 CUPS HOME-COOKED OR CANNED RED KIDNEY BEANS

CHOPPED SCALLIONS, FOR SERVING

SHREDDED CHEDDAR CHEESE, FOR SERVING

1. Heat the oil in the stockpot over medium-high heat. Add the beef, pork, onions and garlic and cook, stirring constantly, until the meats lose all pink color.

2. Stir together the chili powder, salt, cumin and oregano. Stir the mixture into the meats. Add the stock, beer, tomato sauce, tomatoes and beans. Simmer, uncovered, stirring now and then, for 1 hour.

3. Skim off any floating fat from the top of the chili. Transfer the chili to the buffet. Offer bowls of scallions and cheese on the side.

Skip's Chili

My cousin, Harry Dyck (a.k.a. Skip), is a captain in the Navy. From his letter that accompanied this recipe: "By some standards this chili is respectably hot; by Navy standards it is very bland. I usually add 2 jalapeño peppers, seeded and diced, with the tomatoes. If this is still too mild, I offer additional red pepper flakes to liven up individual portions. My last batch was sized to feed 500 hungry sailors and lost little in the expansion."

Handling hot chile peppers with your bare hands can be dangerous. Slip a plastic bag over the hand that will touch the peppers. After working with the peppers, discard the bag and wash your hands with warm soapy water before even thinking of touching your eyes, nose or mouth.

5-quart nonreactive stockpot
Makes 3 quarts/8 moderate servings

5 TABLESPOONS CANOLA OIL
2 POUNDS LEAN BEEF TOP ROUND, CUT INTO ½-INCH CUBES AND
  PATTED DRY
1½ POUNDS LEAN PORK LOIN, CUT INTO ½-INCH CUBES AND
  PATTED DRY
4 GARLIC CLOVES, MINCED
2 LARGE YELLOW ONIONS, COARSELY CHOPPED
¼ CUP CHILI POWDER OR PURE GROUND CHILES

1½ TEASPOONS GROUND OREGANO
1½ TEASPOONS GROUND CUMIN
1 TEASPOON CRUSHED RED PEPPER FLAKES
2 CUPS HOMEMADE BEEF STOCK OR CANNED BROTH
1 CAN (28 OUNCES) WHOLE TOMATOES
1 CAN (6 OUNCES) TOMATO PASTE
1 TABLESPOON SALT (OPTIONAL)
1 TEASPOON SUGAR
1 TO 2 TABLESPOONS CORNMEAL (OPTIONAL)

1. Heat 3 tablespoons of the oil in the stockpot over medium-high heat. Add the beef and pork and cook, stirring constantly, until lightly browned on all sides. Transfer the meats to a bowl.

2. Reduce the heat to medium and add the remaining 2 tablespoons oil to the pot. Add the garlic and onions and cook, stirring often, until the onions are tender, 5 to 7 minutes.

3. Stir in the chili powder, oregano, cumin and red pepper flakes and mix well, coating the onions with the spices. Stir in the stock, tomatoes, tomato paste, salt and sugar. Break up the tomatoes with a spoon. Put the meat and any accumulated juices back into the pot and stir well. Cover and simmer for 1 hour.

4. Uncover and simmer for 40 to 50 minutes longer, or until the meat is very tender. Set aside to cool. Cover and refrigerate overnight.

5. When ready to serve: Slowly bring the chili to a simmer and simmer until heated through. (Be careful lest it burn on the bottom of the pot.) If the chili is too liquid, do not cover the pot. If it is the right consistency, heat it covered. When hot, thicken, if needed, by sprinkling 1 tablespoon of the cornmeal over the chili and cook, stirring constantly, until thickened. Repeat, if necessary. Serve in heavy pottery bowls.

Red Beans and Bacon Chili

This chili uses spicy barbecue sauce to give it a come-back-for-more flavor. It's perfect with corn bread.

5-quart nonreactive stockpot and a large skillet
Makes 3 1/2 quarts/8 hearty servings

1 POUND DRIED RED BEANS, RINSED AND DRAINED

1 POUND LEAN BACON, DICED

1 LARGE YELLOW ONION, CHOPPED

2 POUNDS GROUND CHUCK

1 1/2 CUPS SPICY BARBECUE SAUCE

2 CUPS HOMEMADE BEEF STOCK OR CANNED BROTH

2 TABLESPOONS CHILI POWDER OR PURE GROUND CHILES

1 TABLESPOON STONE-GROUND CORNMEAL

1. Combine the beans and 6 cups of water and soak for 6 to 8 hours or overnight. Alternately, bring the beans and water to a boil. Boil for 2 minutes. Remove from the heat, cover and let stand for 1 hour.

2. Drain the beans. Combine the beans with 6 cups of fresh water in the stockpot and bring to a boil. Reduce the heat to a simmer, cover and cook for 1 hour, or until the beans are tender. Remove from the heat and uncover.

3. In the skillet, cook the bacon over medium heat until crisp. Remove with a slotted spoon and add to the beans.

4. Pour off all but 1 tablespoon of the bacon drippings. Add the onion and cook, stirring often, until tender. Transfer to the beans with a slotted spoon.

5. Add the beef to the skillet and cook, stirring often, until all pink color disappears. Transfer to the beans with a slotted spoon.

6. Stir in the barbecue sauce and stock. Stir together the chili powder and cornmeal; stir into the pot. Bring to a gentle simmer and cook, uncovered, stirring now and then, for 30 minutes. Serve in heavy pottery bowls.

Char-Broiled Chili

Making char-broiled hamburgers for a crowd can leave you with leftover burgers. Don't throw them away—make chili.

3-quart saucepan
Makes 1 1/4 quarts/4 moderate servings

1 TABLESPOON CANOLA OIL
1 YELLOW ONION, CHOPPED
1/2 GREEN BELL PEPPER, SEEDED AND DICED
1 GARLIC CLOVE, MINCED
1 TABLESPOON CHILI POWDER OR PURE GROUND CHILES
1/2 TEASPOON GROUND CUMIN
1/4 TEASPOON GROUND OREGANO
4 LEFTOVER CHAR-BROILED HAMBURGERS (4 OUNCES EACH),
   COOKED MEDIUM RARE TO MEDIUM (*NOT* WELL DONE)
2 CUPS HOME-COOKED OR CANNED RED KIDNEY BEANS
1/2 CUP TOMATO KETCHUP
SALT AND PEPPER, TO TASTE
DILL PICKLE SPEARS, FOR SERVING

1. Heat the oil in the saucepan over medium heat. Add the onion, bell pepper and garlic and cook, stirring often, until the onion is tender, 5 to 7 minutes. Remove from the heat.

2. Sprinkle on the chili powder, cumin and oregano and stir well.

3. Chop the leftover burgers into 1/4-inch dice. Add the burgers to the pot, along with the beans, ketchup and 1/2 cup of water. Simmer, uncovered, stirring often, for 15 minutes.

4. Taste and add salt and pepper, if needed. Serve with a dill pickle spear on the side.

Roadhouse Chili

This chili can be made with ingredients readily available on the grocer's shelf. Serve with saltine crackers and cold soda pop or beer.

3-quart nonreactive saucepan
Makes 2 quarts/6 moderate servings

2 POUNDS GROUND CHUCK
2 GARLIC CLOVES, MINCED
2 TEASPOONS SALT (OPTIONAL)
2 TABLESPOONS CHILI POWDER OR PURE GROUND CHILES
1 TEASPOON GROUND CUMIN
1 TEASPOON GROUND OREGANO
2 TABLESPOONS CANOLA OIL
2 LARGE YELLOW ONIONS, COARSELY CHOPPED
1/4 TEASPOON CRUSHED RED PEPPER FLAKES
1 TABLESPOON WORCESTERSHIRE SAUCE
1 1/2 CUPS CHILI SAUCE (KETCHUP TYPE)
4 CUPS HOME-COOKED OR CANNED RED KIDNEY BEANS

1. Mix the beef with the garlic, salt, chili powder, cumin and oregano.

2. Heat the oil in the saucepan over medium heat. Add the onions and cook, stirring often, until tender, about 7 minutes.

3. Add the meat mixture to the pan and cook, stirring often, until the meat loses all pink color, about 5 minutes.

4. Stir in the red pepper flakes, Worcestershire, chili sauce and kidney beans. Simmer, uncovered, stirring now and then, for 45 minutes. Add a small amount of water if the mixture becomes too dry. Serve in heavy pottery bowls.

Lunch Counter Chili

This is the kind of chili they used to dish up at dime store lunch counters. It's easy and fast and very, very good.

3-quart nonreactive saucepan
Makes 1½ pints/3 moderate servings

1 POUND GROUND CHUCK
¾ TEASPOON SALT (OPTIONAL)
1 TABLESPOON CHILI POWDER OR PURE GROUND CHILES
2 TEASPOONS CANOLA OIL
1 LARGE YELLOW ONION, VERY FINELY CHOPPED
1 CAN (8 OUNCES) TOMATO SAUCE

1. Mix together the beef, salt and chili powder. Heat the oil in the saucepan over medium-high heat. Add the onion and sauté for 2 minutes. Add the beef mixture and cook, stirring, until the beef loses all pink color, 3 to 5 minutes.

2. Stir in the tomato sauce. Reduce the heat and simmer, stirring often, for 10 minutes, or until the meat is cooked through and the chili thickens. Add a small amount of water if the chili gets too thick.

3. Adjust the salt, if necessary. Serve in heavy pottery bowls or on whole-grain hamburger buns.

Spicy Gumbos

From Southern climes

Bless the Cajuns for giving us gumbo. It is true peasant fare, using whatever the cook has at hand. Its potpourri of flavor brings the bayou to the French Quarter. My first trip to New Orleans was as a preteen, tagging along with my mother on a sight-seeing shopping trip. After a morning of taking in the exotic sights, sounds and smells—from the blooming of Jackson Square to the decadence of Bourbon Street—we stopped at The Court of Two Sisters for lunch. I ordered my first bowl of gumbo, and I've been hooked ever since.

End-of-the-Week Gumbo

This gumbo is a catchall kind of a dish. Little dabs of leftover meats—chicken, duck, turkey or ham—can be added to the basic soup to make a tasty meal. If the week has run lean without much in the way of leftovers, simply add another cup of compatible vegetables, such as carrots, celery or green beans.

3-quart nonreactive saucepan
Makes 1½ quarts/4 moderate servings

3 TABLESPOONS CANOLA OIL

1 YELLOW ONION, CHOPPED

1 GARLIC CLOVE, MINCED

2½ TABLESPOONS ALL-PURPOSE FLOUR

1 QUART HOMEMADE CHICKEN STOCK OR CANNED BROTH, HEATED
  UNTIL HOT

2 CUPS FRESH OR FROZEN SLICED OKRA

2 CUPS FRESH OR CANNED CHOPPED TOMATOES

1 CUP DICED LEFTOVER COOKED CHICKEN, DUCK, TURKEY OR HAM

½ BAY LEAF

1 FRESH THYME SPRIG, OR ¼ TEASPOON DRIED

½ TEASPOON WORCESTERSHIRE SAUCE

DASH OF HOT PEPPER SAUCE

SALT AND PEPPER, TO TASTE

HOT COOKED RICE, FOR SERVING (OPTIONAL)

1. Warm 1 tablespoon of the oil in the saucepan over medium heat. Add the onion and the garlic and cook, stirring occasionally, until the onion is tender, 5 to 7 minutes. Remove the onion and the garlic to a dish.

2. Add the flour and the remaining 2 tablespoons oil to the pan and cook over low heat, stirring occasionally, until the mixture turns light tan. Add the stock, increase the heat and cook, stirring, until the mixture comes to a boil. Reduce the heat to a simmer and add the reserved onions and garlic. Stir in the okra, tomatoes, leftover meat, bay leaf, thyme, Worcestershire and hot pepper sauce. Cover and cook at a very low simmer for 1 hour.

3. Remove the bay leaf. Taste and add salt and pepper, if needed. Place about ¼ cup of the rice in each bowl. Ladle the soup over the rice.

North of New Orleans Gumbo

One wintry day, hungry for the flavors of the French Quarter, I devised a recipe for a seafood gumbo that could be made with items available on a Midwestern grocer's shelf. The first afternoon I made it, my daughter's piano teacher was in the house for a lesson. As she left through the kitchen door, she took a deep breath and said, "Do you people eat this well all the time?"

5-quart nonreactive stockpot
Makes 2 quarts/6 moderate servings

3 SLICES LEAN BACON, DICED
CANOLA OIL
1/4 CUP ALL-PURPOSE FLOUR
1 QUART HOMEMADE CHICKEN STOCK, CLAM JUICE STOCK OR
    CANNED BROTH, HEATED UNTIL HOT
2 CUPS CANNED TOMATOES
1 GARLIC CLOVE, MINCED
2 YELLOW ONIONS, COARSELY CHOPPED
4 CELERY RIBS WITH LEAVES, COARSELY CHOPPED
1 PACKAGE (10 OUNCES) FROZEN SLICED OKRA
1 BAY LEAF
4 FRESH THYME SPRIGS, OR 1/2 TEASPOON DRIED
1/2 TEASPOON CRUSHED RED PEPPER FLAKES
PINCH OF GROUND ALLSPICE
PINCH OF GROUND CLOVES
PINCH OF FRESHLY GRATED NUTMEG
1/2 TEASPOON WORCESTERSHIRE SAUCE
1 CAN (4 1/2 OUNCES) DEVEINED SHRIMP, RINSED AND DRAINED
2 CANS (6 OUNCES EACH) CRABMEAT, RINSED AND DRAINED
SALT AND PEPPER, TO TASTE
COOKED RICE (OPTIONAL)

1. In the stockpot, sauté the bacon over medium heat until almost crisp. Remove the bacon with a slotted spoon and reserve. You should have about 4 tablespoons bacon drippings. Add oil, if necessary, to make up the deficit.

2. Sprinkle the flour over the drippings and cook over low heat, stirring constantly, until the roux begins to turn a coppery brown. Be patient; this could take as long as 30 minutes. Don't be tempted to rush the process by raising the heat.

3. Add the hot stock all at once and stir constantly until the mixture is smooth. Add the reserved bacon and the tomatoes, garlic, onions, celery, okra, bay leaf, thyme, red pepper flakes, allspice, cloves, nutmeg and Worcestershire. Reduce the heat to a simmer, cover and cook for 1 hour, stirring occasionally.

4. Stir in the shrimp and crabmeat and cook at a bare simmer for 15 minutes.

5. Remove the bay leaf. Taste and add salt and pepper, if needed. Serve in large flat soup bowls, with or without the rice.

Ham and Sausage Gumbo

I like to stew a pot of this gumbo when the okra and tomatoes are thick in my garden. It's good with chunks of French bread to sop up the juices.

3-quart nonreactive saucepan
Makes 2 quarts/6 moderate servings

2 TABLESPOONS CANOLA OIL
1 YELLOW ONION, CHOPPED
½ GREEN BELL PEPPER, SEEDED AND DICED
2 CELERY RIBS, DICED
1 GARLIC CLOVE, MINCED
8 OUNCES SMOKED SAUSAGE, SLICED
4 OUNCES HAM, CUBED
3 TABLESPOONS ALL-PURPOSE FLOUR
3 CUPS HOMEMADE CHICKEN STOCK OR CANNED BROTH, HEATED
  UNTIL HOT
3 CUPS FRESH OR FROZEN SLICED OKRA
2 CUPS FRESH OR CANNED CHOPPED TOMATOES
1 TEASPOON CHOPPED FRESH THYME, OR ½ TEASPOON DRIED
¼ TEASPOON CRUSHED RED PEPPER FLAKES
PINCH OF GROUND CLOVES
1 BAY LEAF
SALT AND PEPPER, TO TASTE

1. Heat the oil in the saucepan over medium heat. Add the onion, bell pepper, celery and garlic and cook, stirring often, until the onion is tender, 5 to 7 minutes.

2. Stir in the sausage and ham. Stir in the flour. Add the hot stock and cook, stirring, until thickened. Add the okra, tomatoes, thyme, red pepper flakes, cloves and bay leaf. Cover and simmer for 45 minutes.

3. Remove the bay leaf. Add salt and pepper to taste. Serve in flat soup plates.

Fish House Gumbo

This is a quick gumbo that can be made with fresh or frozen fish fillets. If you use frozen, chop into bite-size pieces before they are fully thawed.

3-quart nonreactive saucepan
Makes 1½ quarts/4 moderate servings

2 TABLESPOONS CANOLA OIL
1 YELLOW ONION, CHOPPED
1 GARLIC CLOVE, MINCED
¼ GREEN BELL PEPPER, SEEDED AND DICED
2 CELERY RIBS, DICED
2 TABLESPOONS ALL-PURPOSE FLOUR
2 CUPS HOMEMADE FISH OR CHICKEN STOCK OR CANNED BROTH,
   HEATED UNTIL HOT
2 CUPS FRESH OR CANNED CHOPPED TOMATOES
2 CUPS FRESH OR FROZEN SLICED OKRA
1 TABLESPOON CHOPPED FRESH PARSLEY
1 TEASPOON CHOPPED FRESH THYME, OR ½ TEASPOON DRIED
¼ TEASPOON HOT PEPPER SAUCE
1 BAY LEAF
1 POUND FISH FILLETS, CUT INTO BITE-SIZE PIECES
SALT AND PEPPER, TO TASTE
COOKED WHITE RICE, FOR SERVING

1. Heat the oil in the saucepan over medium heat. Add the onion, garlic, bell pepper and celery and cook, stirring often, until the onion is tender, 5 to 7 minutes.

2. Stir in the flour. Add the hot stock and cook, stirring, until thickened. Stir in the tomatoes, okra, parsley, thyme, hot pepper sauce and bay leaf. Cover and simmer for 15 minutes.

3. Remove the bay leaf. Add the fish, cover and simmer for 15 minutes.

4. Add salt and pepper to taste. Serve over cooked rice.

Tomato-Okra Gumbo

Gumbo doesn't have to include meats to be good. Add some tasty all-vegetable gumbos to your menus.

3-quart nonreactive saucepan
Makes 2 quarts/6 moderate servings

2 TABLESPOONS CANOLA OIL
1 YELLOW ONION, CHOPPED
1 GARLIC CLOVE, MINCED
3 TABLESPOONS ALL-PURPOSE FLOUR
1 QUART HOMEMADE CHICKEN STOCK OR CANNED BROTH, HEATED UNTIL HOT
2 CARROTS, SLICED
2 CELERY RIBS, SLICED
2 CUPS FRESH OR CANNED CHOPPED TOMATOES
2 CUPS FRESH OR FROZEN SLICED OKRA
1 CUP FRESH OR FROZEN CORN KERNELS
1 TABLESPOON CHOPPED FRESH PARSLEY
1 TEASPOON CHOPPED FRESH THYME, OR ½ TEASPOON DRIED
1 TEASPOON CHOPPED FRESH MARJORAM, OR ¼ TEASPOON DRIED
SALT AND PEPPER, TO TASTE

1. Heat the oil in the saucepan over medium heat. Add the onion and garlic and sauté until the onion is tender, 5 to 7 minutes.

2. Stir in the flour. Add the hot stock and cook, stirring, until thickened. Stir in the carrots, celery, tomatoes, okra, corn, parsley, thyme and marjoram. Cover and simmer for 30 minutes.

3. Add salt and pepper, to taste. Serve in heavy pottery bowls.

Sweet Potato Gumbo

Nothing could be more southern than a sweet potato gumbo. Serve with Sweet Milk Corn Bread (page 202).

3-quart nonreactive saucepan
Makes 2 quarts/6 moderate servings

1 TEASPOON CANOLA OIL
1 YELLOW ONION, CHOPPED
1 QUART HOMEMADE CHICKEN STOCK OR CANNED BROTH
3 SWEET POTATOES (ABOUT 2 POUNDS), PEELED AND DICED
2 CUPS FRESH OR FROZEN SLICED OKRA
2 CUPS FRESH OR FROZEN GREEN PEAS
2 CUPS FRESH OR CANNED CHOPPED TOMATOES
1 TEASPOON CHOPPED FRESH THYME, OR ½ TEASPOON DRIED
DASH OF HOT PEPPER SAUCE
SALT AND PEPPER, TO TASTE

1. Heat the oil in the saucepan over medium heat. Add the onion and cook, stirring often, until tender, 5 to 7 minutes.
2. Add the stock, sweet potatoes, okra, peas, tomatoes, thyme and hot pepper sauce. Cover and simmer for 30 minutes.
3. Add salt and pepper to taste. Serve in heavy pottery bowls.

Gumbo Z'Herbes

Gumbo Z'Herbes should be made with a variety of early greens and herbs. The flavors blend together in the cooking to make a perfect spring tonic. Cooked ham or sausages can be added at the last to make the dish more substantial.

5-quart nonreactive stockpot
Makes 1½ quarts/4 moderate servings

4 SLICES LEAN BACON, DICED
2 POUNDS FRESH YOUNG GREENS, SELECTED FROM: SPINACH,
    SORREL, LEAF LETTUCE, COLLARDS, MUSTARD, RADISH TOPS, BEET
    TOPS, CARROT TOPS, TURNIP TOPS, DANDELION TOPS,
    WATERCRESS, TOUGH STEMS REMOVED
1 SMALL HEAD OF CABBAGE (ABOUT 1 POUND), COARSELY
    CHOPPED
2 QUARTS COLD WATER
GENEROUS HANDFUL (12 SPRIGS) OF FRESH HERBS SELECTED FROM:
    THYME, PARSLEY, SAGE, DILL, TARRAGON, CHIVES, FENNEL
2 YELLOW ONIONS, CHOPPED
3 GARLIC CLOVES, MINCED
3 TABLESPOONS ALL–PURPOSE FLOUR
1 TABLESPOON CIDER VINEGAR
1 TEASPOON SALT (OPTIONAL)
PINCH OF CAYENNE PEPPER
PINCH OF CRUSHED RED PEPPER FLAKES
PINCH OF GROUND ALLSPICE
COOKED BROWN OR WHITE RICE, FOR SERVING

1. In the stockpot, cook the bacon over medium heat until crisp. Drain on paper towels and reserve. Pour off and reserve the drippings.

2. Combine the greens, cabbage and cold water in the pot. Bring to a boil. Reduce the heat to a simmer, cover and cook until the greens are tender, about 20 minutes. Drain, reserving the cooking liquid.

3. Combine the greens and herbs in a food processor. Pulse to chop, but do not puree. Alternately, chop with a knife. Reserve.

4. Rinse and dry the pot. Add 2 tablespoons of the reserved bacon drippings and warm over medium heat. Add the onions and garlic and sauté until the onions are tender, 5 to 7 minutes.

5. Stir in the flour. Stir in 4 cups of the reserved cooking liquid. Cook, stirring, until thickened. Stir in the vinegar, salt, cayenne, red pepper flakes and allspice. Stir in the reserved greens and bacon. Simmer, stirring, until thick and saucy. Add more of the cooking liquid if the sauce is too thick. Serve over hot rice.

Comforting Cream Soups

Harmonious flavors

I use the term "cream" advisedly. Often as not light cream is all the richness needed. Sometimes skim milk suffices. My choices are based on my own palate. Feel free to adjust the recipes to reflect your own, substituting heavier milks or creams as you will. Some of the soups are thinned purees. They sometimes cross the line into creamed, which is why I have combined them in this chapter. I have also included soups thickened with pureed cooked rice. They have the texture of a creamed soup but are not creamed in the traditional sense. They do let us enjoy the comfort of creamed food with very little fat.

Herb Garden Soup

Use only fresh herbs in this soup. It's best made right before serving, so the herbs retain their fresh appeal.

3-quart saucepan
Makes 5 cups/6 appetizer servings

3 TABLESPOONS UNSALTED BUTTER
3 TABLESPOONS ALL-PURPOSE FLOUR

1 QUART HOMEMADE CHICKEN STOCK OR CANNED BROTH, HEATED
  UNTIL HOT
½ CUP CHOPPED FRESH PARSLEY
¼ CUP CHOPPED FRESH CHIVES
2 TABLESPOONS CHOPPED FRESH HERBS OF YOUR CHOICE: THYME,
  LEMON THYME, TARRAGON, MARJORAM, FENNEL OR ROSEMARY
1 CUP LIGHT OR HEAVY CREAM
SALT AND WHITE PEPPER, TO TASTE

1. Melt the butter in the saucepan over medium-low heat. Add the flour and cook, stirring, for 3 minutes. Add the hot stock, stirring all the while. Cook over medium heat, stirring, until thickened and smooth.

2. Stir in the parsley, chives and other herbs. Cover and simmer for 5 minutes.

3. Stir in the cream. Heat through, but do not boil. Add salt and pepper, to taste. Serve in small soup cups.

Chicken Velvet

This is a wonderful, restorative soup. It has a smooth, creamy base, filled with satisfying little pieces of perfectly poached chicken.

3-quart saucepan
Makes 1 quart/4 appetizer or 2 moderate servings

2 CUPS HOMEMADE CHICKEN STOCK OR CANNED BROTH
1 SMALL YELLOW ONION, PEELED AND STUCK WITH 1 WHOLE
  CLOVE
1 BAY LEAF
1 BONELESS, SKINLESS CHICKEN BREAST (ABOUT 8 OUNCES)
4 TABLESPOONS UNSALTED BUTTER
1/4 CUP ALL-PURPOSE FLOUR
2 CUPS SKIM MILK OR LIGHT CREAM, SCALDED
2 TABLESPOONS CHOPPED FRESH PARSLEY
SALT AND WHITE PEPPER, TO TASTE
FRESHLY GRATED NUTMEG, FOR SERVING

1. In the saucepan, combine the stock, onion, bay leaf and chicken breast. Simmer gently, with the lid slightly ajar, for 15 minutes. Remove from the heat and let stand for 5 minutes.

2. Strain the mixture, reserving the stock and chicken separately. Discard the clove-studded onion and bay leaf. As soon as the chicken is cool enough to handle, chop into very small dice, 1/4-inch or less. Add the chicken to the reserved stock.

3. Rinse and dry the saucepan. Add the butter and melt over medium heat. Sprinkle on the flour and cook, stirring, for 2 minutes. Add the scalded milk and cook, stirring constantly, until thickened. Gradually stir in the stock and chicken. Stir in the parsley. Heat through, but do not boil.

4. Taste and add salt and pepper, if needed. Serve in white bowls, if available. Dust each serving lightly with freshly grated nutmeg.

Cream of Asparagus Soup

Asparagus is one of my favorite vegetables. I decided I wanted to grow my own patch so that I could have fresh (and free) spears whenever I wanted them, rather than pay a dear price for what I might find at the market.

I looked in my gardening encyclopedia to see how to accomplish my task and read what seemed to me to be an awful lot of work. I was to dig trenches a foot deep and 18 inches wide. In these trenches I was to form a mound of composted earth to about half the depth of the trench. Then I could purchase 1-year asparagus roots, which I was to drape over the piled earth. Next the soil had to be shoveled back into the trenches to cover the tips of the new plants by 2 or 3 inches. Gradually, as the spears grew that first year, the soil needed to be shoveled in to cover them, until the surface of the bed was even again. If I was lucky, I might be able to start harvesting asparagus for kitchen use the second year after planting.

I'm not afraid of work, but anything that takes longer than one afternoon disinterests me. Besides, asparagus comes up volunteer in right-of-ways beside fields where roots have been planted, their seeds having blown there by the wind. Wouldn't it do at least that much for me, if I gave it a little help?

Ignoring the "formal instruction," I purchased a packet of seeds and prepared my seedbed. I marked off the rows and scattered the seeds along them. I then raked the soil gently, just enough to cover the seeds. That's about all I did the first year, except for an occasional weeding. A moderate mulch of straw keeps the roots covered and is slowly elevating the bed. Although I am the ultimate optimist, the resulting crops have exceeded my wildest expectations. Whenever I have a little extra, I like to make this uncomplicated soup for lunch. I like the simplicity of combining the asparagus puree with the béchamel sauce for a fresh-from-the-garden flavor.

3-quart saucepan
Makes 1 1/2 quarts/4 moderate servings

2 POUNDS ASPARAGUS, THINLY SLICED
2 CUPS HOMEMADE CHICKEN STOCK OR CANNED BROTH
4 TABLESPOONS UNSALTED BUTTER
1/4 CUP ALL-PURPOSE FLOUR
3 CUPS SKIM MILK, SCALDED AND HOT
SALT AND WHITE PEPPER, TO TASTE

1. Combine the asparagus and stock in the saucepan. Simmer, covered, until the asparagus is tender, about 15 minutes.
2. Transfer the soup to a food processor and puree.
3. Rinse and dry the saucepan. Melt the butter over medium heat. Add the flour and cook, stirring often, for 2 to 3 minutes. Add the hot milk and stir vigorously over medium heat until the mixture thickens. Gradually stir in the asparagus puree. Taste and add salt and pepper, if needed. Serve with whatever crackers or breads are at hand.

Sunchoke Soup Supreme

Sunchokes, or Jerusalem artichokes, are native North American perennial sunflowers. It is the tuber at the base of the plant that is used for food. When freshly dug after frosts have sharpened their flavor, they need only be scrubbed with a brush. No peeling is required.

two 3-quart saucepans
Makes 1 1/2 quarts/6 appetizer servings

1 POUND SUNCHOKES, SCRUBBED AND SLICED
4 CUPS COLD WATER
2 TABLESPOONS FRESH LEMON JUICE
4 TABLESPOONS UNSALTED BUTTER

¼ CUP ALL-PURPOSE FLOUR

1 QUART HOMEMADE CHICKEN STOCK OR CANNED BROTH, HEATED
  UNTIL HOT

SALT AND WHITE PEPPER, TO TASTE

1 CUP LIGHT OR HEAVY CREAM

FRESHLY GRATED NUTMEG, FOR SERVING

1. Combine the sunchokes, cold water and lemon juice in a sauce-pan and bring to a boil. Reduce the heat, cover and simmer until the chokes are tender, 30 to 45 minutes. Remove the pan from the heat; uncover.

2. Melt the butter in the second saucepan. Stir in the flour and cook over low heat for 5 minutes, stirring frequently. Add the hot stock and cook, stirring, until smooth and thickened.

3. Drain the sunchokes. Puree in a blender or food processor. Stir the puree into the thickened stock. Season to taste with salt and pepper. Heat, stirring frequently, until almost boiling. Stir in the cream and heat through, but do not boil.

4. Ladle the soup into bowls and dust each serving with the freshly grated nutmeg.

Tureen of Turnips

This combination of root vegetables produces a richly flavored puree. Be sure to use young turnips. The large older ones can be overpowering. I like this with dainty sandwiches made with thinly sliced, buttered rye.

3-quart saucepan
Makes 1½ quarts/4 moderate servings

1½ QUARTS HOMEMADE BEEF STOCK OR CANNED BROTH
1 POUND SMALL TURNIPS, PEELED AND CHOPPED
1 YELLOW ONION, CHOPPED
1 CARROT, CHOPPED
1 MEDIUM RUSSET OR WHITE POTATO, PEELED AND DICED
4 TABLESPOONS UNSALTED BUTTER
¼ CUP ALL-PURPOSE FLOUR
SALT AND WHITE PEPPER, TO TASTE
DRY SHERRY, FOR PASSING AT THE TABLE

1. In the saucepan, combine the stock, turnips, onion, carrot and potato. Cover and simmer until the vegetables are tender, about 30 minutes.

2. Drain the vegetables, reserving the stock. Puree the vegetables in a food processor or blender and reserve.

3. Rinse and dry the saucepan. Melt the butter in the pan. Add the flour and cook over medium heat, stirring frequently, until cooked but not browned, about 4 minutes. Off the heat, add the reserved stock, stirring all the while. Return the pot to medium heat and cook, stirring occasionally, until thickened to the consistency of very thin gravy.

4. Stir in the pureed vegetables. Heat until almost boiling, stirring often. Add salt and pepper to taste. Serve at the table from a decorative tureen. Ladle into warm pottery bowls. Pass a cruet of the sherry for diners to add according to individual taste.

Cream of Summer Soup

I usually use green zucchini for this soup, but it works equally well with a yellow crookneck variety. Try some of each.

5-quart stockpot
Makes 2 1/2 quarts/8 moderate servings

2 TABLESPOONS EXTRA–VIRGIN OLIVE OIL
1 YELLOW ONION, CHOPPED
8 CUPS FINELY CHOPPED UNPEELED SUMMER SQUASH
1 QUART HOMEMADE CHICKEN STOCK OR CANNED BROTH
1 TABLESPOON MINCED FRESH SUMMER SAVORY (THERE IS NO
   DRIED SUBSTITUTE; IF NOT AVAILABLE LEAVE IT OUT.)
1 TABLESPOON MINCED FRESH PARSLEY
3 TABLESPOONS CORNSTARCH
1 CUP SKIM MILK
SALT AND WHITE PEPPER, TO TASTE
THIN LEMON SLICES, FOR GARNISH

1. Warm the olive oil in the stockpot over medium–high heat. Add the onion and sauté until tender, 3 to 5 minutes. Stir in the squash. Cover and cook over medium heat for 10 minutes, stirring 2 or 3 times during the cooking. Remove the pot from the heat.

2. With a slotted spoon, remove 2 cups of the cooked squash. Puree through a sieve or in a blender or food processor. Return the puree to the pot of soup.

3. Stir in the chicken stock, summer savory and parsley. Bring to a gentle boil. Reduce the heat to a simmer.

4. Dissolve the cornstarch in the milk. Stir the milk mixture into the soup and cook, stirring frequently, until the soup thickens, 2 to 3 minutes. Add salt and pepper to taste. Serve hot in small bowls or soup cups. Float a lemon slice on top of each serving.

Cream of Mushroom Soup

I make this soup with common button mushrooms, but when I have morels, I mix in one or two to add a woodsy flavor.

3-quart saucepan
Makes 1 quart/4 appetizer servings

3 TABLESPOONS UNSALTED BUTTER
8 OUNCES FRESH BUTTON MUSHROOMS, SLICED
1 YELLOW ONION, FINELY CHOPPED
1 TABLESPOON CHOPPED FRESH PARSLEY
3 TABLESPOONS ALL-PURPOSE FLOUR
2 CUPS HOMEMADE CHICKEN STOCK OR CANNED BROTH, HEATED
  UNTIL HOT
1 CUP LIGHT CREAM
SALT AND WHITE PEPPER, TO TASTE
CHOPPED FRESH CHIVES, FOR GARNISH

1. Melt the butter in the saucepan over medium heat. Add the mushrooms, onion and parsley and cook, stirring often, until the mushrooms and onion are tender, 7 to 10 minutes.

2. Stir in the flour. Stir in the hot stock and cook, stirring, until thickened. Process in a food processor to a coarse puree.

3. Return the soup to the pot. Stir in the cream. Heat through, but do not boil. Taste and add salt and pepper, if needed. Sprinkle each serving with the chives.

Cream of Cauliflower Soup

When beautiful creamy-white heads of cauliflower come into season, I want to cook them every way I can, and this is one of our favorites.

two 3-quart saucepans
Makes 2 quarts/6 moderate servings

1 LARGE HEAD OF CAULIFLOWER, SEPARATED INTO FLORETS
1 TEASPOON FRESH LEMON JUICE

BOILING WATER
¼ CUP FINELY CHOPPED ONION
4 TABLESPOONS UNSALTED BUTTER
¼ CUP ALL-PURPOSE FLOUR
1 QUART HOMEMADE CHICKEN STOCK OR CANNED BROTH, HEATED
  UNTIL HOT
2 CUPS SKIM MILK OR LIGHT CREAM, SCALDED
SALT AND WHITE PEPPER, TO TASTE
FRESHLY GRATED NUTMEG, FOR GARNISH
CHOPPED FRESH PARSLEY, FOR GARNISH

1. In a saucepan, cook the cauliflower with the lemon juice in just enough boiling water to cover until tender, 7 to 10 minutes. Drain.

2. Meanwhile, combine the onion and butter in the other saucepan over medium heat. Cook until the onion is tender, 5 to 7 minutes.

3. Stir the flour into the onions. Add the hot stock and cook, stirring, until thickened.

4. Puree the cauliflower in a food processor or blender. Stir the puree into the soup. Stir in the scalded milk and heat through.

5. Taste and add salt and pepper, if needed. Serve in small bowls. Dust with the nutmeg and sprinkle a stripe of chopped parsley across the center of each serving.

Carrot Vichyssoise

Classic vichyssoise (pronounced veeshee-swahz) is a simple soup of leeks and potatoes, thinned with fresh cream and chilled before serving. The most famous version was created by the late Louis Diat during the time he was chef at the Ritz-Carlton in New York City. The name, vichyssoise, can be used for any cold soup based on potatoes and another vegetable. I like this version, flavored with carrots, and the next, made with beets. Both can be eaten hot or cold.

3-quart saucepan
Makes 5 cups/4 moderate servings

2 CUPS HOMEMADE CHICKEN STOCK OR CANNED BROTH
2 MEDIUM RUSSET OR WHITE POTATOES, PEELED AND DICED
3 MEDIUM CARROTS, DICED
1 LEEK (WHITE PART ONLY), SLICED
2 CUPS SKIM MILK OR LIGHT CREAM
1 TEASPOON CHOPPED FRESH DILL, OR ½ TEASPOON DRIED
SALT AND WHITE PEPPER, TO TASTE
RAW CARROT STRIPS, FOR GARNISH
LIGHT CRÈME FRAÎCHE, FOR SERVING COLD (RECIPE FOLLOWS)

1. Combine the stock, potatoes, carrots and leek in the saucepan. Cover and simmer for 30 minutes, or until the vegetables are soft.

2. Puree the soup in a food processor or blender. Return to the saucepan and stir in the milk and dill. Heat through, but do not boil.

3. Add salt and pepper to taste. Serve hot in small soup cups, garnished with curled carrot strips. To serve cold, chill for several hours. Taste and adjust the seasonings before serving. Serve in small cups, nestled in bowls of cracked ice. Top with a dollop of Light Crème Fraîche and place a carrot curl on top of that.

Light Crème Fraîche

This is a shortcut version for making crème fraîche with flavor that comes from lowfat sour cream.

no-cook
Makes 2 cups

1 CUP HEAVY CREAM, CHILLED
1 CUP LIGHT (LOWFAT) SOUR CREAM, CHILLED

1. Gradually stir the cream into the sour cream. Whisk or beat with a hand-held beater until slightly thickened.

2. Cover and refrigerate. Will keep, chilled, for about 7 days.

Beet Vichyssoise

In this soup, the potatoes soften the beet flavor, while taking advantage of their rosy hue.

3-quart nonreactive saucepan
Makes 5 cups/4 moderate servings

2 CUPS HOMEMADE BEEF STOCK OR CANNED BROTH
2 MEDIUM RUSSET OR WHITE POTATOES, PEELED AND DICED
1 LEEK (WHITE PART ONLY), SLICED
1 CELERY RIB, DICED
1 CAN (8 OUNCES) SLICED BEETS, DRAINED
2 CUPS SKIM MILK OR LIGHT CREAM
SALT AND WHITE PEPPER, TO TASTE
CHOPPED FRESH CHIVES, FOR GARNISH
LIGHT CRÈME FRAÎCHE (PRECEDING RECIPE), FOR SERVING COLD

1. Combine the stock, potatoes, leek and celery in the saucepan. Cover and simmer for 30 minutes, or until the vegetables are soft. Remove from the heat.

2. Stir in the beets. Puree the mixture in a food processor. Taste, and if the soup is not perfectly smooth, press through a sieve with a wooden spoon.

3. Return the puree to the pot. Stir in the milk and heat through, but do not boil.

4. Add salt and pepper, if needed. Serve hot in small bowls, garnished with the chives. To serve cold, chill for several hours. Taste and

adjust the seasonings. Serve in small soup cups, nestled in bowls of cracked ice. Swirl a spoonful of Light Crème Fraîche into each serving. Scatter the chives on top.

Curried Cream of Potato Soup

This simple soup makes a delicious lunch on a cold winter day. Whole wheat crackers and hot applesauce round out the meal.

3-quart saucepan
Makes 1½ quarts/4 moderate servings

3 CUPS HOMEMADE CHICKEN, BEEF OR VEGETABLE STOCK OR CANNED BROTH
1 GARLIC CLOVE, MINCED
1 SMALL YELLOW ONION, FINELY CHOPPED
3 CUPS PEELED AND DICED RUSSET OR WHITE POTATOES
1 CUP SKIM MILK OR LIGHT CREAM
1 TEASPOON CURRY POWDER
2 TABLESPOONS UNSALTED BUTTER, SOFTENED
SALT AND WHITE PEPPER, TO TASTE
CHOPPED FRESH PARSLEY, FOR GARNISH

1. In the saucepan, combine the stock, garlic, onion and potatoes. Cover and simmer until the potatoes begin to fall apart, 45 to 60 minutes. Remove from the heat.

2. Put the mixture through a sieve or puree in a food processor or blender. Return to the pot.

3. Stir in the milk, curry powder and butter. Heat until hot, but do not boil. Add salt and pepper to taste. Sprinkle each serving with fresh parsley.

Cream of Sweet Potato Soup

This is better than sweet potatoes fixed any other way.

3-quart saucepan
Makes 1 1/2 quarts/6 appetizer servings

3 SWEET POTATOES (ABOUT 2 POUNDS), PEELED AND CUBED
2 CUPS HOMEMADE CHICKEN STOCK OR CANNED BROTH
1/8 TEASPOON GROUND CLOVES
ABOUT 1 1/2 CUPS SKIM MILK OR LIGHT CREAM
SALT AND WHITE PEPPER, TO TASTE
FRESHLY GRATED NUTMEG, FOR SERVING

1. Combine the sweet potatoes and stock in the saucepan. Cover and simmer for 20 minutes, or until the sweet potatoes are tender. Process in a food processor or run through a food mill to puree. Return to the rinsed and dried pan.

2. Stir in the 1 1/2 cups of milk. Heat through but do not boil. Thin with additional milk or cream, if needed. Add salt and pepper, to taste. Dust each serving lightly with freshly grated nutmeg.

Cream of Rice Soup

The white rice provides a creamy base for this soup, and the brown or wild rice adds a complementary texture and flavor. For a different outcome, you can substitute chopped cooked vegetables or chicken for the rice in the bowl.

3-quart saucepan
Makes 1 ½ quarts/4 moderate servings

2 TABLESPOONS EXTRA-VIRGIN OLIVE OIL
1 YELLOW ONION, CHOPPED
¼ CUP DICED CARROT
¼ CUP DICED CELERY
4 CUPS HOMEMADE BEEF STOCK OR CANNED BROTH
1 FRESH MARJORAM OR OREGANO SPRIG (IF AVAILABLE)
⅓ CUP UNCOOKED WHITE RICE
2 CUPS SKIM MILK OR LIGHT CREAM
SALT AND WHITE PEPPER, TO TASTE
1 CUP HOT, COOKED BROWN OR WILD RICE, FOR SERVING
CHOPPED FRESH PARSLEY, FOR GARNISH

1. Heat the oil in the saucepan over medium heat. Add the onion, carrot and celery and cook, with the lid slightly ajar, stirring now and then, until tender, 7 to 10 minutes.

2. Stir in the stock, marjoram and white rice. Simmer, covered, for 30 minutes, or until the rice is very tender.

3. Puree in a food processor or blender. Return the puree to the saucepan.

4. Stir in the milk. Heat through, but do not boil. Taste and add salt and pepper, if desired. Place ¼ cup brown or wild rice in each serving bowl. Ladle in the hot soup. Garnish with the parsley.

Tomato "Rice" Soup

This is a high-carbohydrate, lowfat "cream" of tomato soup. If you make it with the skim milk, it's positively skinny.

3-quart nonreactive saucepan
Makes 1 ½ quarts/4 moderate servings

2 CUPS HOMEMADE CHICKEN STOCK OR CANNED BROTH
1 CAN (8 OUNCES) TOMATO SAUCE
⅓ CUP UNCOOKED WHITE RICE
2 TABLESPOONS MINCED ONION
1 TABLESPOON CHOPPED FRESH PARSLEY
1 TABLESPOON CHOPPED FRESH BASIL (DON'T USE DRIED. IF FRESH
  ISN'T AVAILABLE, DOUBLE THE PARSLEY.)
2 CUPS SKIM MILK OR LIGHT CREAM, SCALDED
SALT AND WHITE PEPPER, TO TASTE
PEELED, SEEDED, CHOPPED FRESH TOMATO, FOR GARNISH

1. Combine the stock, tomato sauce, rice, onion, parsley, basil and 1 cup of water in the saucepan. Simmer, covered, for 30 minutes, or until the rice is very tender.

2. Puree in a food processor. Return to the pot.

3. Slowly add the milk, stirring all the while. Season to taste with salt and pepper. (The soup can be reheated, but do not boil.) Serve in soup cups, garnished with chopped fresh tomato.

Creamy Peanut Butter Soup

If you are familiar with my previous books, you know that I adore peanut butter. It's perfect in this curry-seasoned soup.

3-quart saucepan
Makes 4½ cups/6 appetizer servings

1 TABLESPOON CANOLA OIL
1 TABLESPOON UNSALTED BUTTER
1 SMALL YELLOW ONION, FINELY CHOPPED
½ CELERY RIB, FINELY DICED
2 TABLESPOONS ALL-PURPOSE FLOUR
¾ TEASPOON CURRY POWDER
PINCH OF CRUSHED RED PEPPER FLAKES
2 CUPS SKIM MILK OR LIGHT CREAM, SCALDED
¾ CUP CREAMY PEANUT BUTTER
2 CUPS HOMEMADE CHICKEN STOCK OR CANNED BROTH
SALT AND WHITE PEPPER, TO TASTE
CHOPPED DRY-ROASTED PEANUTS, FOR GARNISH

1. Heat the oil with the butter in the saucepan over medium heat. Add the onion and celery and sauté until the onion is tender, 5 to 7 minutes.

2. Stir together the flour, curry powder and red pepper flakes. Stir the mixture into the pot. Add the scalded milk and cook, stirring, until thickened. Remove from the heat.

3. Measure the peanut butter into a bowl. Gradually stir in the cooked onion-milk mixture. Stir in the stock. Strain through a sieve. Cover and refrigerate until chilled.

4. When ready to serve, taste and add salt and pepper, if needed. Scatter chopped peanuts in the center of each serving.

Creamy Cheese and Onion Soup

This is thick and creamy and very cheesy. If you're on a diet, you'd better make something else.

3-quart nonstick or regular saucepan
Makes 2 quarts/6 moderate servings

4 TABLESPOONS UNSALTED BUTTER
2 YELLOW ONIONS, CHOPPED
¼ CUP ALL-PURPOSE FLOUR
4 CUPS SKIM MILK, SCALDED
½ TEASPOON CELERY SEEDS
1 CUP LIGHT CREAM
1 SMALL PACKAGE (3 OUNCES) CREAM CHEESE, CUT INTO SMALL
   PIECES
2 CUPS (8 OUNCES) GRATED SHARP CHEDDAR CHEESE
SALT AND WHITE PEPPER, TO TASTE
CHOPPED FRESH CHIVES, FOR GARNISH

1. Melt the butter in the saucepan over medium heat. Add the onions and sauté until tender, 5 to 7 minutes.

2. Stir in the flour. Add the scalded milk and cook, stirring constantly, until thickened. Stir in the celery seeds, cream and cheeses. Continue to cook, stirring gently, until the cheeses melt. Do not allow to burn.

3. Add salt and pepper to taste. Garnish the servings with the chives.

Calico Cheese Soup

If you don't overcook them, the carrots and celery add a nice textural contrast to the melted cheese.

3-quart nonstick or regular saucepan
Makes 2 quarts/6 moderate servings

2 TABLESPOONS UNSALTED BUTTER
2 TABLESPOONS EXTRA-VIRGIN OLIVE OIL
1 SMALL YELLOW ONION, FINELY CHOPPED
1 CELERY RIB, DICED
1 CARROT, DICED
¼ CUP ALL-PURPOSE FLOUR
¾ TEASPOON POWDERED MUSTARD
2 CUPS HOMEMADE CHICKEN STOCK OR CANNED BROTH, HEATED
   UNTIL HOT
2 CUPS SKIM MILK
2 CUPS LIGHT CREAM
¼ CUP (2 OUNCES) DICED BOTTLED PIMIENTOS, DRAINED
2 CUPS (8 OUNCES) SHREDDED SHARP CHEDDAR CHEESE
2 TABLESPOONS GRATED PARMESAN CHEESE
SALT AND WHITE PEPPER, TO TASTE

1. Melt the butter with the oil in the saucepan. Add the onion, celery and carrot and sauté until the onion is tender and the celery and carrots are crisp-tender, 5 to 7 minutes.

2. Sprinkle the flour and powdered mustard over the vegetables and stir to mix. Stir in the hot stock and cook, stirring, until thickened. Stir in the milk, cream and pimientos. Heat through, but do not boil.

3. Add the cheeses and cook, stirring gently, until melted. Taste and add salt and pepper, if needed. Serve in heavy pottery bowls.

Cream of Macaroni and Cheese Soup

This soup evokes old-fashioned macaroni and cheese—it's wonderful.

two 3-quart saucepans
Makes about 5 cups/4 moderate servings

164

2 CUPS HOMEMADE CHICKEN STOCK OR CANNED BROTH
4 OUNCES (ABOUT 1 CUP) SMALL SHELL MACARONI
3 TABLESPOONS UNSALTED BUTTER
1 SMALL YELLOW ONION, CHOPPED
3 TABLESPOONS ALL-PURPOSE FLOUR
2 CUPS SKIM MILK OR LIGHT CREAM, SCALDED
2 CUPS (8 OUNCES) SHREDDED SHARP CHEDDAR CHEESE
SALT AND WHITE PEPPER, TO TASTE
CHOPPED FRESH PARSLEY, FOR GARNISH

1. In one of the saucepans, bring the stock to a boil. Drop in the macaroni, regulate the heat to a simmer, cover and cook, stirring often, for 7 minutes. Do not drain when cooked; remove from the heat.

2. Meanwhile, melt the butter in the other saucepan over medium heat. Add the onion and sauté until tender, 5 to 7 minutes.

3. Sprinkle the flour over the onion and cook for 1 minute longer. Add the scalded milk and cook, stirring, until thickened.

4. Add the cooked macaroni and any remaining stock. Stir in the cheese and cook, stirring gently, until melted. (This is supposed to be a thick soup, but it can be too thick. Thin with stock, milk or cream, if needed.) Add salt and pepper, to taste. Garnish each serving with the parsley.

Cream of Salmon Soup

A simple onion-flavored white sauce forms the basis for this satisfying salmon soup.

two 2-quart saucepans
Makes 1½ quarts/4 moderate servings

4 TABLESPOONS UNSALTED BUTTER
1 TABLESPOON FINELY CHOPPED ONION
¼ CUP ALL-PURPOSE FLOUR
2 CUPS SKIM MILK
2 CUPS LIGHT CREAM
1 CAN (16 OUNCES) RED SALMON, MEAT FLAKED AND LIQUID
   RESERVED
SALT AND WHITE PEPPER, TO TASTE
CHOPPED FRESH PARSLEY, FOR GARNISH

1. Melt the butter in the saucepan over low heat. Add the onion and cook until translucent, about 3 minutes. Blend in the flour and cook, stirring, for 1 minute longer.

2. Scald the milk and the cream together in another pot.

3. Add the scalded liquids to the onion mixture and cook, stirring constantly, until the mixture thickens.

4. Add the salmon and its liquid. Heat through, but do not boil. Add salt and pepper to taste. Sprinkle each serving with the parsley.

Cream of Carbonara Soup

I was in an Italian restaurant, lazily looking over the menu, when it struck me that a wonderful soup could be made with the ingredients described for Pasta Carbonara. And here it is—good with Italian bread and a salad of lettuce, tomatoes, cucumbers and red onion rings, dressed with an Italian dressing.

3-quart saucepan and a large skillet
Makes 1½ quarts/4 moderate servings

2 CUPS SKIM MILK
2 CUPS LIGHT CREAM
1/3 CUP DRY BREAD CRUMBS
1 TEASPOON CHOPPED FLAT-LEAF ITALIAN PARSLEY
8 OUNCES THICK-SLICED BACON, CUT INTO BITE-SIZE PIECES
1 TABLESPOON EXTRA-VIRGIN OLIVE OIL
1 GARLIC CLOVE, MINCED
1 YELLOW ONION, FINELY CHOPPED
8 OUNCES BUTTON MUSHROOMS, SLICED
1/4 CUP FRESHLY GRATED PARMESAN CHEESE
SALT AND WHITE PEPPER, TO TASTE

1. Combine the milk, cream, bread crumbs and parsley in the saucepan. Bring to a gentle, almost not quite there, simmer, and cook, stirring often, while you prepare the remaining ingredients.

2. In the skillet, cook the bacon over medium heat until crisp. Remove with a slotted spoon and drain on paper towels.

3. Spoon off all but 1 tablespoon of the rendered bacon drippings. Add the oil to the skillet. Add the garlic, onion and mushrooms and cook over medium-high heat, stirring often, until the onion and mushrooms are limp and cooked, about 3 minutes.

4. Add the contents of the skillet to the soup and stir. Add the bacon and Parmesan and cook, stirring, just until heated through; do not allow to boil. Taste and add salt and pepper, if needed. Serve in heavy pottery bowls.

Fresh Tomato Bisque

The flavors of fresh garden tomatoes and fresh basil combine to make this light summer soup.

3-quart nonreactive saucepan and a small saucepan
Makes 1 1/2 quarts/4 moderate servings

2 1/2 POUNDS FRESH GARDEN TOMATOES
1 CUP HOMEMADE CHICKEN STOCK OR CANNED BROTH
1 TEASPOON SUGAR
1 TEASPOON SALT
2 TABLESPOONS CHOPPED FRESH BASIL (IF AVAILABLE; DO NOT USE DRIED)
2 CUPS LIGHT CREAM
1 CUP SKIM MILK
4 TABLESPOONS UNSALTED BUTTER
1/4 CUP ALL-PURPOSE FLOUR
WHITE PEPPER, TO TASTE
FRESH BASIL SPRIGS, FOR GARNISH

1. Remove the blossom and stem ends from the tomatoes. Cut the tomatoes into chunks. Combine the tomatoes, stock, sugar and salt in the larger saucepan and bring to a boil. Reduce the heat to a simmer, cover and cook until the tomatoes are very soft, about 30 minutes.

2. Press the mixture through a sieve with the back of a wooden spoon; discard the solids. Stir the basil into the tomato puree; reserve.

3. In the small saucepan, scald the milk and cream over medium heat.

4. Rinse out and dry the larger saucepan. Melt the butter over medium heat. Add the flour and cook, stirring, for 2 to 3 minutes. Add the hot scalded liquids to the butter-flour mixture and stir constantly until smooth.

5. Stir in the reserved tomato puree. Cook, stirring frequently, until heated through; do not allow to boil. Taste and add salt and white pepper, if desired. Serve hot in small bowls or soup cups. Garnish each serving with a fresh basil sprig.

Perfect Cream of Pumpkin Soup

Most pumpkin soups are flavored like a traditional—and sweet—pumpkin pie. I find the gentle spiciness of this soup to be much more satisfying. It's a good first course for a meal that features a turkey loaf or galantine.

3-quart saucepan
Makes 1 quart/4 appetizer servings

2 TABLESPOONS UNSALTED BUTTER
3 TABLESPOONS FINELY CHOPPED SHALLOTS
2 TABLESPOONS ALL–PURPOSE FLOUR
1 CUP SKIM MILK, SCALDED AND HOT
½ TEASPOON CURRY POWDER
2 CUPS HOMEMADE OR CANNED PUMPKIN PUREE
1 CUP HOMEMADE CHICKEN STOCK, CANNED BROTH OR SKIM MILK
SALT AND WHITE PEPPER, TO TASTE

1. Melt the butter in the saucepan over medium-high heat. Add the shallots and cook, stirring frequently, until limp. Sprinkle on the flour and cook for 2 to 3 minutes, stirring frequently. Pour in the hot milk and cook, stirring, until the mixture thickens.
2. One at a time, stir in the curry powder, pumpkin and stock. Bring almost to a boil, stirring often. Add salt and pepper, to taste. Serve hot in small soup cups.

Herbed Green Pea Soup

This is simple to make. I like it as a first course before broiled chicken or fish.

3-quart saucepan
Makes 5 cups/6 appetizer servings

2 CUPS HOMEMADE CHICKEN STOCK OR CANNED BROTH
3½ CUPS SHELLED FRESH PEAS, OR 1 LARGE PACKAGE (16 OUNCES)
   FROZEN GREEN PEAS
2 TABLESPOONS MINCED ONION
2 CUPS LIGHT CREAM
1 TEASPOON CHOPPED FRESH TARRAGON, MARJORAM OR PARSLEY
   (DO NOT USE DRIED)
SALT AND WHITE PEPPER, TO TASTE
FRESH SPRIGS OF THE SAME HERB USED IN THE SOUP, FOR GARNISH

1. Combine the stock, peas and onion in the saucepan. Cover and simmer until the peas are tender.

2. Puree the soup in a food processor. Return the puree to the pot.

3. Add the cream and herb of your choice. Heat through, stirring gently, but do not boil. Add salt and pepper, to taste. Garnish with the herb sprigs.

Fruit Soups

With nature's sweetness

Fruit soups take me back to my Grandmother Nachtigal's kitchen. When I came to visit, I knew I would find cold fruit soup waiting in her refrigerator to be enjoyed with her double-decker zweibach rolls. Soft and wonderful, the rolls were served plain, not buttered, and were as cold as the soup itself. I still think cold rolls are good with chilled fruit combinations.

Rhubarb Soup

Our dining table is positioned so that we can view several gardens at once. We love to watch our brown thrashers in their apparent search for food, as they furiously dig tiny craters in those gardens, sending our mulch flying in the process.

The arrival of brown thrashers to our gardens coincides with the availability of garden rhubarb for kitchen use. So it was that I "had lunch" today with a pair of thrashers, as I enjoyed my first bowl of this season's rhubarb soup.

3-quart nonreactive saucepan
Makes 3 cups/4 dessert servings

3 CUPS THINLY SLICED RHUBARB
¾ CUP SUGAR
¼ CUP DRY WHITE WINE

1. Combine the rhubarb and ½ cup of water in the saucepan. Cover and simmer until the rhubarb is completely tender, about 5 minutes.

2. Stir in the sugar. Cook, stirring, just until the sugar dissolves. Chill the rhubarb mixture.

3. When ready to serve, stir in the wine. Serve in clear glass soup cups.

Plum Perfect Soup

I like to keep a quart of this soup on hand when plums are in season. It gives me a real pick-me-up to have a bowl for a snack. It's also good with simple vanilla cookies for dessert.

3-quart nonreactive saucepan
Makes 2½ quarts/12 snack or dessert servings

2 POUNDS RED PLUMS OR A MIXTURE OF RED AND BLACK (NOT
    PRUNE PLUMS)
1 CUP SUGAR
2 TABLESPOONS CORNSTARCH
4 CUPS COLD WATER
JUICE AND GRATED ZEST OF 1 LEMON
FRESH BASIL SPRIGS, FOR GARNISH

1. Wash, pit and slice the plums. Combine the plums with 4 cups of water in the saucepan. Bring to a boil. Reduce the heat to a simmer and

cook, stirring occasionally, until the plums are completely soft, 30 to 45 minutes.

2. Remove the pan from the heat. Put the pulp through a food mill or puree in a blender or food processor. Return the puree to the pan.

3. Combine the sugar and cornstarch. Mix into the cold water. Stir the sugar mixture into the puree. Place the pan over medium-high heat and bring to a boil, stirring often. Reduce the heat to a simmer and cook, stirring, until the mixture loses its cloudy look, 2 to 3 minutes.

4. Remove the pot from the heat. Continue to stir, skimming off any foam that remains on the top. Stir in the lemon juice and zest.

5. Transfer the soup to quart-size jars and chill. Serve in chilled cups, with basil sprigs for garnish.

Tart Apricot Soup

Apricots with good flavor are available for such a short time that I always try to preserve some of their goodness with this soup. One batch goes into my current menu and one goes into the freezer to enjoy out of season. I like this a little on the tart side. Add additional sugar if it's too tart for your taste.

3-quart nonreactive saucepan
Makes 1½ quarts/6 breakfast or appetizer servings

2 POUNDS RIPE APRICOTS, HALVED AND PITTED
¾ CUP SUGAR
½ TEASPOON GROUND CINNAMON
¼ CUP FRESH ORANGE JUICE
¼ CUP FRESH LEMON JUICE
THIN LEMON SLICES, FOR GARNISH

1. Combine the apricots and 1 cup of water in the saucepan. Cover and simmer for 15 to 20 minutes, or until the apricots are soft.

2. Puree the mixture in a food processor or blender. Stir together

the sugar and cinnamon. Blend into the puree. Blend in the orange and lemon juices.

    3. Cover and refrigerate until chilled. Serve in small glass bowls garnished with the lemon slices.

Nectarine Kiss

This is the easiest soup I know of and it is a delight. Diners should be instructed to eat the fruit first and then drink the wine, which will have been kissed with the flavor of the nectarines.

no-cook
Makes as much as desired

1 FULLY RIPE NECTARINE PER PERSON TO BE SERVED
FRUITY CALIFORNIA CHARDONNAY WINE, AS NEEDED

    1. Use stemmed saucer-shaped Champagne glasses for serving. For each serving, slice 1 fully ripe nectarine and place in one of the glasses. Pour just enough wine over the fruit to cover.

    2. Chill until serving time.

Mango Sunrise

Serve this soup at breakfast with hot muffins.

no-cook
Makes 1 quart/4 breakfast servings

3 RIPE MANGOES (ABOUT 2½ POUNDS)
2 CUPS FRESH ORANGE JUICE

2 TO 4 TABLESPOONS FRESH LEMON JUICE
FRESH NASTURTIUMS, FOR GARNISH (BE SURE THEY ARE
    PESTICIDE–FREE)

1. Peel the mangoes. Cut the fruit from the seeds in chunks. Puree the pulp in a food processor or blender. Blend in the orange juice and 2 tablespoons of the lemon juice. Add additional lemon juice to taste.

2. Cover and refrigerate until chilled. Serve in glass cups with a fresh nasturtium perched at the top.

Strawberry Soup

This soup is perfect with a flute of chilled Champagne for a first course or as dessert.

3-quart nonreactive saucepan
Makes 1 1/2 quarts/8 appetizer or dessert servings

3 CUPS CRUSHED FRESH STRAWBERRIES
1 CUP ORANGE JUICE
3/4 CUP SUGAR
2 TABLESPOONS CORNSTARCH
1/4 CUP COLD WATER
SPRIGS OF FRESH MINT, FOR GARNISH
SLICED FRESH STRAWBERRIES, FOR GARNISH

1. Combine the strawberries, orange juice, sugar and 1 cup of water in the saucepan. Simmer, stirring often, until the sugar dissolves.

2. Stir the cornstarch into the cold water. Stir the mixture into the soup. Cook, stirring, until the soup thickens, about 2 minutes.

3. Chill the soup. Serve in small bowls, garnished with the mint and sliced strawberries.

Honeydew Chiller

This is simply ripe melon and fresh lime juice. Very refreshing at breakfast, brunch or dinner. If you like to salt your melon, you'll want to use it here. If you don't, you won't.

no-cook
Makes 1 quart/4 appetizer servings

1 RIPE HONEYDEW MELON, PARED, SEEDED AND CUBED
ABOUT 1/4 CUP FRESH LIME JUICE, TO TASTE
1/8 TEASPOON SALT (OPTIONAL)
THIN LIME SLICES, FOR GARNISH

1. Puree the melon in a food processor or blender. Blend in the lime juice. Add the salt, if using.
2. Refrigerate until chilled. Serve in small soup cups, garnished with a slice of lime.

Blueberry Soup

When blueberries are in season, we can't seem to get enough. One of our favorite ways to enjoy the blue beauties is in this rum-flavored soup.

3-quart nonreactive saucepan
Makes 2 quarts/8 appetizer or dessert servings

4 CUPS FRESH BLUEBERRIES
3/4 CUP SUGAR
JUICE OF 1 LEMON
1/4 CUP LIGHT RUM
3 TABLESPOONS CORNSTARCH

½ CUP COLD WATER
VANILLA–FLAVORED LOWFAT YOGURT, FOR TOPPING

1. In the saucepan, combine 4 cups of water with the blueberries, sugar, lemon juice and rum. Bring to a gentle boil. Reduce the heat to a simmer, cover and cook for 2 to 3 minutes, or until the fruit is tender.

2. Stir the cornstarch into the cold water. Stir into the soup. Simmer, stirring constantly, until thickened, 2 to 3 minutes.

3. Chill the soup. Serve in small bowls with a dollop of vanilla yogurt.

Sour Cherry Soup

This old-fashioned recipe uses lemon extract rather than fresh lemon juice. I've tried it both ways and the extract is a delicious choice.

3-quart nonreactive saucepan
Makes 1 quart/5 dessert servings

4 CUPS PITTED FRESH–PICKED SOUR CHERRIES
1 CUP SUGAR
2 TABLESPOONS CORNSTARCH
½ CUP COLD WATER
1 TEASPOON PURE LEMON EXTRACT

1. Stir the cherries and the sugar together in the saucepan. Cook over medium heat, stirring often, until the cherries are tender.

2. Stir the cornstarch into the cold water. Add to the pot. Cook, stirring constantly, until the mixture thickens, about 2 minutes. Remove from the heat. Stir in the lemon extract. Serve warm or cold.

Elderberry Soup

We have planted elderberries in our yard as part of our natural bird feed. They are prolific enough for man and feathered friend to share. To provide elderberries for your birds and stockpot, plant more than one variety. Cross pollination will double your crop.

3-quart nonreactive saucepan
Makes 5 cups/6 appetizer or dessert servings

1 POUND ELDERBERRIES (SEE STEP 1)
3 TABLESPOONS CORNSTARCH
¼ CUP COLD WATER
JUICE AND GRATED ZEST OF 2 LEMONS
1 CUP SUGAR
6 FRESH MINT SPRIGS

1. Wash the elderberries and strip them from the clusters. You should have about 4 cups of berries. In the saucepan, combine the elderberries with 4 cups of water. Bring to a boil. Reduce the heat to a simmer and cook, with the lid slightly ajar, until the fruit is soft, about 20 minutes.

2. Remove the pan from the heat. Put the pulp through a food mill, or press through a sieve with a wooden spoon. Clean the saucepan of any residue that adheres to the sides. Return the sieved pulp to the clean pan.

3. Stir the cornstarch into the cold water. Add to the pot, along with the lemon juice, lemon zest and sugar. Bring just to a simmer and cook for about 3 minutes, or until thickened.

4. Chill. Serve in small cups with a mint sprig for garnish.

Pumpernickel–Apple Soup
(Apfelbrotsuppe)

I know my German heritage leads me to try ideas like this, but you don't have to be German to enjoy it. Serve with pumpernickel-bread-and-butter sandwiches.

3-quart nonreactive saucepan
Makes 5 cups/4 moderate servings

4 LARGE, TART COOKING APPLES, PEELED, CORED AND SLICED
1 QUART HOMEMADE CHICKEN STOCK OR CANNED BROTH
3 SLICES PUMPERNICKEL BREAD, CRUSTS REMOVED
1/4 CUP RAISINS
2 TABLESPOONS BROWN SUGAR
1 TABLESPOON FRESH LEMON JUICE
GRATED ZEST OF 1 LEMON
1/4 TEASPOON GROUND CINNAMON

1. Combine the apples and stock in the saucepan. Tear the bread into pieces and drop into the pot. Cook at a simmer, covered, until the apples are soft, 20 to 30 minutes.

2. Puree the mixture through a food mill or in a food processor or blender. Return to the pan.

3. Stir in the raisins, sugar, lemon juice, lemon zest and cinnamon. Simmer, covered, until the raisins are plump, about 5 minutes. Serve in rustic pottery bowls.

Curried Apple Soup

Curry is the perfect flavoring for this assertive apple soup. If I have leftover cooked chicken or turkey, I dice some and add it to the hot version for a substantial lunch.

3-quart saucepan
Makes 2 quarts/6 moderate servings

1 TABLESPOON EXTRA-VIRGIN OLIVE OIL
1 TABLESPOON UNSALTED BUTTER
1 YELLOW ONION, CHOPPED
4 LARGE TART COOKING APPLES, PEELED, CORED AND SLICED
1½ TEASPOONS CURRY POWDER
1 QUART HOMEMADE BEEF STOCK OR CANNED BROTH
1½ CUPS SKIM MILK OR LIGHT CREAM
SALT AND PEPPER, TO TASTE
FINELY CHOPPED PARSLEY OR APPLES, FOR GARNISH

1. Heat the oil and butter in the saucepan over medium heat. Add the onion and cook, stirring often, until tender, 5 to 7 minutes.

2. Add the apples. Sprinkle with the curry and cook, stirring, for 3 minutes longer. Add the stock and bring to a boil. Reduce the heat to a simmer and cook, covered, until the apples are tender, about 15 minutes.

3. Puree the soup in batches in a food processor or blender. Return to the saucepan. Add the milk and heat, but do not boil. This soup is good hot or cold. If served hot, use the parsley garnish, if cold, the apple.

Applesauce Soup

This is easy to make during any season. It's perfect with molasses cookies.

3-quart nonreactive saucepan
Makes 1¾ quarts/6 dessert servings

4 CUPS HOMEMADE OR CANNED UNSEASONED APPLESAUCE
3¼ CUPS APPLE CIDER OR JUICE
¼ CUP SUGAR
1 TABLESPOON CORNSTARCH
1 TEASPOON GROUND CINNAMON
⅛ TEASPOON GROUND CLOVES
1 TABLESPOON UNSALTED BUTTER, SOFTENED
1 TABLESPOON FRESH LEMON JUICE
FRESHLY GRATED NUTMEG, FOR SERVING

1. Combine the applesauce and 3 cups of the apple cider in the saucepan. Bring to a simmer, stirring now and then.
2. In a bowl, stir together the sugar, cornstarch, cinnamon and cloves. Stir in the remaining ¼ cup apple cider. Stir the sugar mixture into the pot and cook, stirring, until thickened, 1 to 2 minutes. Remove from the heat.
3. Gently stir in the butter and then the lemon juice. Chill. Serve in small bowls with a dusting of nutmeg.

Tropical Fruit Soup

You can play around with this recipe. Use fresh pineapple when in season. Sliced kiwi, seedless grapes or star fruit can be added or substituted for some of the other fruits. It's refreshing for dessert, or serve with a muffin for a light, healthful breakfast.

no-cook
Makes 1 quart/4 breakfast or 6 dessert servings

2 CUPS SLICED FRESH STRAWBERRIES
2 CUPS SLICED BANANAS
1 CAN (8 OUNCES) CRUSHED PINEAPPLE PACKED IN ITS OWN JUICE
1 CUP FRESH ORANGE JUICE
2 TABLESPOONS FRESH LEMON JUICE
2 TABLESPOONS HONEY
FRESH MINT OR BASIL SPRIGS, FOR GARNISH

1. Combine all of the fruits in a large bowl. Stir together the pineapple and citrus juices and the honey and pour over the fruit. Stir gently to coat all pieces. Cover with plastic wrap and chill.
2. Serve in glass cups. Garnish with sprigs of mint or basil.

Curried Fruit Soup

A touch of curry brings out the flavor of summer apricots, plums and nectarines. This is good with plain butter cookies.

3-quart nonreactive saucepan
Makes 2 quarts/8 dessert servings

1 CUP SUGAR
3/4 TEASPOON CURRY POWDER
1/4 TEASPOON GROUND CINNAMON
1 POUND APRICOTS, PITTED AND SLICED
1 POUND RED PLUMS, PITTED AND SLICED
1 POUND NECTARINES, PITTED AND SLICED
1 TABLESPOON UNSALTED BUTTER, SOFTENED
1 TABLESPOON FRESH LEMON JUICE

1. Stir together the sugar, curry powder and cinnamon in the saucepan. Stir in 2 cups of water, the apricots, plums and nectarines. Bring to a simmer, stirring now and then, and cook, covered, for 15 minutes, or until the fruit is tender.

2. Stir in the butter and lemon juice. Refrigerate until chilled. Serve in small bowls.

Jelled Scandinavian Fruit Soup

This is a refreshing variation of the standard fruit compote. It doesn't become overly sweet like some stewed dried fruit does. Serve it with buttered crackers for an appetizer or with sugar cookies for dessert.

3-quart nonreactive saucepan
Makes 1½ quarts/8 appetizer or dessert servings

1 CUP PITTED PRUNES
1 CUP DRIED APRICOTS
1 CUP DRIED PEACHES
1 CUP GOLDEN RAISINS
1 BOX (3 OUNCES) LEMON-FLAVORED GELATIN
⅛ TEASPOON GROUND CINNAMON
⅛ TEASPOON GROUND CLOVES
1 CUP BOILING WATER

1. Combine 3 cups of water with the prunes, apricots, peaches and raisins in the saucepan. Let stand, covered, for 1 hour.

2. Bring the fruit mixture to a simmer and cook, covered, for 15 minutes, or until the fruit is tender. Remove from the heat.

3. In a bowl, stir together the gelatin, cinnamon and cloves. Stir in the boiling water until the gelatin dissolves. Stir the gelatin mixture into the fruit. Pour into an 8-inch square glass dish. Chill until jelled.

Corner-Cutting Soups

Surprisingly good

Very few people have time to cook from scratch during the week. Single-parent households and households with two working adults allow for quick recipes at best. So that you don't have to wait for the weekend to enjoy a good bowl of soup, I have devised some very quick soups made from items that can be kept on hand in your pantry. Although many of these soups start with a can of condensed soup, they have flavorings and combinations that take them a step above merely opening a can and heating. Serve them as attractively as you would a dish you make from scratch. When you receive compliments on their goodness, simply say "Thank you." There's no need to explain that the concoction came from the opening of cans.

Tomato Sunrise/Sunset

Enjoy this as an eye-opener in the morning or as a beginning course for dinner. Totally refreshing.

no-cook
Makes a little more than 2 1/2 cups/3 breakfast or appetizer servings

1 CAN (10¾ OUNCES) CONDENSED TOMATO SOUP
1 SOUP CAN ORANGE JUICE
PEPPER, TO TASTE
FRESH ORANGE SLICES, FOR GARNISH

1. Place the soup in a deep bowl. Gradually stir in the orange juice. Taste and add pepper, if desired.
2. Serve cold, in clear glass cups, garnished with the orange slices.

Bombay Chiller

Serve this in small soup cups as a first course for dinner.

no-cook
Makes 2¾ cups/3 to 4 appetizer servings

1 CAN (10¾ OUNCES) CONDENSED CREAM OF CHICKEN SOUP
½ TEASPOON CURRY POWDER
1 TEASPOON FRESH LEMON JUICE
1 TABLESPOON DRY SHERRY
1 SOUP CAN SKIM MILK OR LIGHT CREAM
STORE-BOUGHT CHUTNEY, FOR GARNISH

1. In a bowl, stir together the chicken soup, curry powder, lemon juice and sherry. Chill for at least 1 hour.
2. When ready to serve, stir in the milk. Garnish each serving with a dollop of the chutney.

Mongolian Puree

This is super-simple and exceptionally good.

2-quart saucepan
Makes 5 cups/4 moderate servings

1 CAN (10¾ OUNCES) CONDENSED TOMATO SOUP
1 CAN (10¾ OUNCES) CONDENSED CREAM OF GREEN PEA SOUP
1 TEASPOON RED WINE VINEGAR
PINCH OF MACE
PINCH OF GROUND GINGER
PINCH OF GROUND CINNAMON
2 SOUP CANS HOT WATER
GARLIC CROUTONS (SEE PAGE 211), FOR GARNISH

1. In the saucepan, stir together the soups, the vinegar and the spices. Gradually stir in the hot water. Heat until hot, but not boiling.
2. Garnish the servings with the croutons.

Devilish Cheese Soup

Serve this soup with fresh fruit and whole wheat rolls for a satisfying meal.

1-quart saucepan
Makes 3 cups/2 moderate servings

1 CAN (10¾ OUNCES) CONDENSED CHEDDAR CHEESE SOUP
1 CAN (4¼ OUNCES) DEVILED HAM
1 SOUP CAN SKIM MILK OR LIGHT CREAM
1 TEASPOON CHOPPED FRESH PARSLEY
1 TEASPOON DRIED MINCED ONION

1. In the saucepan, stir together all of the ingredients. Heat until hot, but do not boil. Serve immediately.

Cheesy Cream of Broccoli Soup

Serve with a mixed citrus salad for a satisfying supper.

2-quart nonstick saucepan
Makes 5½ cups/4 moderate servings

2 CANS (10¾ OUNCES EACH) CONDENSED CREAM OF BROCCOLI
   SOUP
2 SOUP CANS SKIM MILK
1 CUP (4 OUNCES) SHREDDED LOWFAT CHEDDAR CHEESE
¼ CUP GRATED PARMESAN CHEESE
FRESHLY GRATED NUTMEG, FOR GARNISH

1. Place the soup in the saucepan. Gradually stir in the milk. Add the cheeses and cook over medium heat, stirring, just until melted.
2. Dust each serving with the grated nutmeg.

Hot Beet Borsch

This tasty appetizer soup is very low in calories.

2-quart nonreactive saucepan
Makes 3 1/2 cups/4 appetizer servings

1 CAN (16 OUNCES) DICED BEETS, UNDRAINED
1 CAN (ABOUT 13¾ OUNCES) BEEF BROTH
1 TABLESPOON MINCED DRIED ONION
1 TEASPOON SUGAR
2 TEASPOONS RED WINE VINEGAR

1. In the saucepan, combine all of the ingredients and bring just to a boil. Serve in small soup cups.

Chilled Cranberry Borsch

Serve this lovely pink borsch at holiday time.

no-cook
Makes 5 cups/6 appetizer servings

1 CAN (16 OUNCES) SLICED BEETS, UNDRAINED
1 CAN (16 OUNCES) JELLIED CRANBERRY SAUCE
½ CUP FRESH ORANGE JUICE
2 TABLESPOONS FRESH LEMON JUICE
1 CUP LOWFAT PLAIN YOGURT, PLUS MORE FOR GARNISH

1. Puree the beets and their liquid with the cranberry sauce in a food processor or blender. Transfer to a bowl.

2. Stir in the orange juice and lemon juice. Stir 1 cup of the yogurt until smooth; stir into the soup. Cover and refrigerate until chilled.

3. Serve in small glass soup cups. Swirl a spoonful of yogurt into each serving.

Tart Tomato Soup

The tart taste of the yogurt is a perfect match for the tomato.

1-quart nonreactive saucepan
Makes 2½ cups/2 moderate servings

1 CAN (10¾ OUNCES) CONDENSED TOMATO SOUP
¼ CUP SKIM MILK OR WATER
1 CUP LOWFAT PLAIN YOGURT
1 TEASPOON CHOPPED FRESH DILL, OR ½ TEASPOON DRIED

1. In the saucepan, stir together the soup and milk. Stir in the yogurt and dill. Heat until hot, but do not boil. Serve immediately.

Celery-Cheese Soup

Serve with chilled pears for a wonderful lunch or light supper.

2-quart nonstick saucepan
Makes 5½ cups/4 moderate servings

2 CANS (10¾ OUNCES EACH) CREAM OF CELERY SOUP
2 SOUP CANS SKIM MILK
½ TEASPOON DILL SEEDS
¼ TEASPOON POWDERED MUSTARD
1 CUP (4 OUNCES) SHREDDED LOWFAT MONTEREY JACK CHEESE
FRESH DILL SPRIGS, WHEN AVAILABLE, FOR GARNISH

1. Place the soup in the saucepan. Gradually stir in the milk. Stir in the dill seeds and powdered mustard. Heat until hot, but not boiling.
2. Stir in the cheese and heat just until melted. Garnish each serving with a dill sprig.

Beanie Weenie Tomato Soup

The kids will love this.

2-quart saucepan
Makes 5 cups/3 moderate servings

1 CAN (11½ OUNCES) BEAN WITH BACON CONDENSED SOUP
1 CAN (10¾ OUNCES) CONDENSED TOMATO SOUP
4 FULLY COOKED LOWFAT FRANKFURTERS, SLICED DIAGONALLY
1 TABLESPOON DRIED MINCED ONION
½ TEASPOON CHILI POWDER
¼ TEASPOON GROUND CUMIN
SHREDDED LOWFAT CHEDDAR CHEESE, FOR GARNISH

1. In the saucepan, stir together the soups, frankfurters, onion, chili powder, cumin and 2 cups of water. Cook until the frankfurters are heated through.
2. Garnish each serving with the shredded cheese.

Cheesy Clam Chowder

This is surprisingly good for as fast as it is.

1-quart nonstick saucepan
Makes 3 cups/2 moderate servings

1 CAN (10¾ OUNCES) CONDENSED CREAM OF POTATO SOUP
1 CAN (6½ OUNCES) CHOPPED OR MINCED CLAMS, DRAINED
¾ CUP SKIM MILK OR LIGHT CREAM
1 TABLESPOON DRIED MINCED ONION
½ CUP (2 OUNCES) SHREDDED LOWFAT MONTEREY JACK CHEESE
CRUMBLED CRISP BACON, FOR GARNISH

1. In the saucepan, stir together the soup, clams, milk and onion. Bring almost to a boil.

2. Stir in the cheese and heat just until melted. Garnish each serving with the crumbled bacon.

Crabmeat Bisque

For a quick supper on a cold winter's evening, this can't be beat.

2-quart saucepan
Makes 3 1/2 cups/2 moderate servings

1 CAN (10¾ OUNCES) CONDENSED CREAM OF CHICKEN SOUP
1 CAN (6 OUNCES) CRABMEAT, RINSED AND DRAINED
1 SOUP CAN SKIM MILK OR LIGHT CREAM
1 TABLESPOON DRY SHERRY
CHOPPED FRESH PARSLEY, FOR GARNISH

1. In the saucepan, stir together the soup, crabmeat and milk. Heat through.

2. Add the sherry and heat until hot, but do not boil. Garnish each serving with the chopped parsley.

Shrimp Bisque

Substitute 1 can (4½ ounces) deveined shrimp, rinsed and drained, for the crabmeat. Proceed as before.

Creamy Corn and Bacon Soup

This quick and easy soup goes well with Nuthin' Muffins (page 205).

2-quart saucepan
Makes 5 cups/3 moderate servings

3 SLICES LEAN BACON, DICED
2 CUPS FROZEN OR WELL-DRAINED CANNED WHOLE KERNEL CORN
1 CAN (10¾ OUNCES) CONDENSED CREAM OF CELERY SOUP
1½ SOUP CANS SKIM MILK OR LIGHT CREAM

1. In the saucepan, sauté the bacon over medium-high heat until almost crisp. Spoon out all but 1 tablespoon of the drippings.
2. Reduce the heat to medium. Add the corn and cook, partially covered, stirring now and then, for 5 minutes, or until just beginning to brown. Remove from the heat.
3. Stir in the soup and then the milk. Return to medium-high heat and cook, stirring, until just heated through.

Beer–Cheese Soup

This makes a perfect lunch. Serve with warmed pretzels.

3-quart saucepan
Makes 2 quarts/6 moderate servings

3 CANS (11 OUNCES EACH) CONDENSED CHEDDAR CHEESE SOUP
2 SOUP CANS SKIM MILK OR LIGHT CREAM
1 CAN (12 OUNCES) BEER
DASH OF HOT PEPPER SAUCE
¼ TEASPOON POWDERED MUSTARD
WHITE PEPPER, TO TASTE

1. In the saucepan, stir together the soup, milk, beer, hot pepper sauce and powdered mustard. Bring to a simmer, stirring often.

2. Taste and add white pepper, if desired. Serve in bowls or beer mugs.

Breads and Crackers

A few special recipes

It was my love for bread that got me started in teaching and writing about home-style cooking. Even though I have written two books on breads, I still come up with new recipes all of the time. Here are a few that I especially like to serve with soup.

Whole-Grain French Bread

This recipe uses a wet sponge technique for starting the bread dough. I find it a surefire way to add an old-world flavor to the loaf.

Large baking sheet
Makes 2 loaves

SPONGE:

2 CUPS WARM WATER
2 CUPS STONE-GROUND WHOLE WHEAT FLOUR
1 PACKAGE ACTIVE DRY YEAST

1. In a mixing bowl, stir or whisk the ingredients together. Cover with plastic wrap and let stand for at least 30 minutes or for as long as 12 hours.

BREAD:

¾ TEASPOON SALT

1 TABLESPOON EXTRA-VIRGIN OLIVE OIL

ABOUT 3 CUPS UNBLEACHED ALL-PURPOSE FLOUR

OLIVE OIL, FOR THE BOWL

CORNMEAL, FOR THE BAKING SHEET

1 LARGE EGG WHITE

1 TEASPOON COOL WATER

2. Stir the salt, the oil and 1 cup of the flour into the sponge. Beat well. Gradually stir in the remaining 2 cups flour to make a soft dough. Toss on a floured surface until no longer sticky. Knead gently for about 5 minutes, or until smooth and elastic, adding flour only to prevent sticking.

3. Place the dough in a bowl coated with about 1 teaspoon olive oil and turn the dough once to oil the top. Cover with plastic wrap and let rise until doubled in bulk, about 1 hour. Sprinkle a large baking sheet liberally with cornmeal.

4. Punch down the dough and divide in half. Working with one half at a time, roll out to a 6 × 12-inch rectangle. Starting with a 12-inch side, roll into a long loaf and place, seam side down, on one side of the prepared baking sheet. When both loaves are formed, place the baking sheet in a cold oven. Place a flat pan filled with hot water below the loaves. Close the oven door and let the dough rise until almost doubled in bulk, 30 to 45 minutes.

5. Remove the loaves and the pan of hot water from the oven. Preheat the oven to 400°F. Lightly beat the egg white with the cool water, and use the mixture to brush the tops of the loaves. Use kitchen shears to cut slashes in the tops of the loaves in 4 to 6 places.

6. Bake the loaves in the preheated oven for 30 minutes. Turn the oven off but let the loaves remain with the door closed for an additional 10 minutes. Cool on wire racks.

FOOD PROCESSOR TIP: Prepare the sponge as in Step 1. For the bread: Use the plastic kneading blade. Place the flour, oil and salt in the food processor bowl. Add the sponge and process until a ball of dough forms on the blade. Proceed as before.

Potato Sponge Light Bread

I know you won't believe this, but I go into the kitchen after our Thanksgiving feast to make potato bread with the water I have saved from boiling the potatoes. My friends tell me they do not intend to follow suit. So, for them, and for you, I have written this recipe to use that same water to make a sponge. You can make it into bread after you've had a day of rest.

two 9 × 5-inch loaf pans
Makes 2 loaves

SPONGE:
2 CUPS WARM POTATO WATER
2 CUPS UNBLEACHED ALL-PURPOSE FLOUR
1 PACKAGE ACTIVE DRY YEAST

1. In a mixing bowl, stir or whisk the ingredients together. Cover with plastic wrap and let stand at room temperature for up to 24 hours.

BREAD:
¼ CUP CANOLA OIL
1 TEASPOON SALT
2 TABLESPOONS SUGAR
ABOUT 4 CUPS UNBLEACHED ALL-PURPOSE FLOUR

2. Add the oil, salt and sugar to the sponge. Gradually add the flour and stir to make a stiff dough. Knead on a floured surface until smooth and elastic.

3. Place the dough in a bowl coated with about 1 teaspoon olive oil and turn the dough once to oil the top. Cover with plastic wrap and let rise until doubled in bulk, about 1 hour.

4. Punch down the dough and divide in half. Shape each half into an oblong loaf. Place each in a well-greased 9 × 5-inch loaf pan. Cover with plastic and let rise until nearly doubled, about 1 hour.

5. Preheat the oven to 350°F.

6. Bake the loaves for 35 to 40 minutes, or until the loaves sound hollow when tapped on the bottoms. Cool on wire racks.

FOOD PROCESSOR TIP: Prepare the sponge as in Step 1. For the bread: Use the plastic kneading blade. Combine the flour (minus 2 tablespoons), sugar and salt in the food processor bowl. Add the olive oil and sponge. Process until a ball of dough forms. If the dough remains too wet, add the reserved 2 tablespoons flour and process again. Proceed as before.

Honey Rye Bread

Some rye doughs are sticky and hard to handle. This one is easy.

9 × 5-inch loaf pan
Makes 1 loaf

2¼ CUPS UNBLEACHED ALL-PURPOSE FLOUR
¾ CUP STONE-GROUND RYE FLOUR
1 TABLESPOON CARAWAY SEEDS
½ TEASPOON SALT
1 CUP WARM WATER
1 PACKAGE ACTIVE DRY YEAST
2 TABLESPOONS CANOLA OIL
2 TABLESPOONS HONEY

1. In a large mixing bowl, stir together the flours, the caraway seeds and salt.

2. In a large measuring cup, use a fork to stir together the warm water and yeast. Stir in the oil and honey. Make a well in the center of the flour mixture and pour the yeast mixture into the well. Gradually stir the flour into the liquid and mix well to form a sticky dough. Cover the bowl with plastic wrap and refrigerate for 30 minutes.

3. Turn out the dough onto a lightly floured surface and press into a 6 × 9-inch rectangle. Starting with a 6-inch side, roll up into a loaf. Place in a well-greased 9 × 5-inch loaf pan. Cover with plastic wrap and let rise for 1 hour, or until doubled.

4. Meanwhile, preheat the oven to 375°F.

5. Cut a shallow slash down the length of the risen loaf. Bake for 35 to 40 minutes, or until the loaf sounds hollow when tapped on the bottom. Cool on a wire rack.

FOOD PROCESSOR TIP: Use the metal blade. Place the flours, the caraway seeds and salt in the workbowl. Pulse to mix. Mix the remainder of the ingredients as before. With the machine running, add the wet ingredients through the feed tube until a sticky dough forms. Proceed as before.

Whole Wheat Batter Bread

If the prospect of kneading bread dough intimidates you, make this batter bread. It stirs up in no time. I give no food processor instructions. Cleanup would take longer than any time saved.

two 9 × 5-inch loaf pans
Makes 2 loaves

2¾ CUPS WARM WATER
2 PACKAGES ACTIVE DRY YEAST
2 TABLESPOONS SUGAR

1½ TEASPOONS SALT
2 TABLESPOONS CANOLA OIL
2 CUPS STONE-GROUND WHOLE WHEAT FLOUR
4 CUPS UNBLEACHED ALL-PURPOSE FLOUR

1. Combine the warm water, yeast and sugar in a large bowl. Let stand for 5 minutes.

2. Stir in the salt, oil and whole wheat flour. Add 2 cups of the all-purpose flour and beat well. Gradually add the remaining 2 cups flour, stirring well. Cover and let rise until doubled in bulk, about 45 minutes.

3. Stir down the batter. Divide between 2 well-greased 9 × 5-inch loaf pans. (It doesn't matter if the dough looks uneven in the pans. It will spread as it rises and will be even by the time it reaches the top.) Cover with oiled plastic and let rise until the batter reaches the top of the pans, 20 to 30 minutes.

4. Meanwhile, preheat the oven to 375°F.

5. Bake the loaves for 35 to 40 minutes, or until each loaf sounds hollow when tapped on the bottom. Cool on wire racks.

Steak House Rolls

There is a restaurant near my home that specializes in steaks. The steaks are good, but it's the rolls that everyone drives miles to enjoy. The restaurant is called The Beef House and it's located in Covington, Indiana, on the northwest corner of the intersection of Interstate 74 and state highway 63. I called to ask if they gave out the recipe for their rolls and talked to manager Glenn Iungerich. He gladly gave me his recipe, but said that it called for 50 pounds of flour, 8 pounds of shortening, 2½ pounds of yeast, ¼ cup salt and 2¾ gallons of water, to be mixed in an 80-quart mixer. Furthermore, he told me that they have their unbleached flour specially ground for them and the shortening they use is not available at retail. He encouraged me to try to cut the recipe down to duplicate the rolls that they serve, but cautioned that I might have to adjust the proportions to achieve my desired results. This is my version of those rolls.

1 or 2 muffin tins
Makes 24 rolls

½ CUP SUGAR
6 TABLESPOONS UNSALTED BUTTER PLUS SOFTENED BUTTER FOR
  THE BOWL AND DOUGH
½ TEASPOON SALT
1 CUP BOILING WATER
½ CUP WARM WATER
2 PACKAGES ACTIVE DRY YEAST
4¼ TO 4½ CUPS UNBLEACHED ALL-PURPOSE FLOUR

1. In a large mixing bowl, stir together the sugar, butter, salt and boiling water until the butter melts. Cool to lukewarm.

2. In a measuring cup, stir together the warm water and yeast to soften the yeast. Add to the sugar mixture and mix well. Add 3 cups of the flour and beat vigorously for 3 minutes. Gradually add the remaining 1¼ to 1½ cups flour and mix to make a soft dough.

3. Turn out the dough on a lightly floured surface and knead until smooth. Transfer to a well-buttered bowl. Smear a little soft butter over the top of the dough. Cover with plastic wrap and let rise for 45 to 60 minutes, or until doubled in bulk.

4. Punch down the dough. Shape into 1¼-inch balls and drop into greased or buttered muffin tins, using 2 balls per muffin cup. Cover and let rise for 30 to 45 minutes, or until a little more than doubled in bulk.

5. Meanwhile, preheat the oven to 400°F.

6. Bake the rolls for 14 minutes, or until lightly browned. Cool on wire racks.

FOOD PROCESSOR TIP: Use the metal blade. Put all of the flour, the salt, sugar and butter in the workbowl. Process until the butter disappears. Soften the yeast in the warm water. Add it to the workbowl. With the machine running, add cool water (in place of boiling) through the feed tube to form a soft dough. Transfer to the buttered bowl and proceed as before.

SHAPING TIP: To shape the balls of dough, push the center of the dough up slightly from the bottom, and then pull the sides down and toward the bottom. This forms better tension for the rising of the rolls than does rolling the dough between your hands or on a board.

Buttermilk Corn Bread

There's no sugar and no egg yolk in this corn bread—and it's delicious!

8-inch square baking dish
Makes 9 servings

1 CUP STONE-GROUND YELLOW CORNMEAL
1 CUP UNBLEACHED ALL-PURPOSE FLOUR
¾ TEASPOON BAKING SODA
¼ TEASPOON SALT
1 CUP BUTTERMILK
2 TABLESPOONS CANOLA OIL
2 LARGE EGG WHITES

1. Preheat the oven to 400°F. Grease an 8-inch square baking dish or spray with cooking spray.

2. In a mixing bowl, stir together the cornmeal, flour, baking soda and salt. Add the buttermilk, oil and egg whites and stir just until the dry particles are moistened; do not overmix. Spoon the batter into the prepared pan.

3. Bake in the preheated oven for 20 to 25 minutes, or until the bread begins to pull away from the sides of the baking dish. Cut into squares and serve warm or cold.

Sweet Milk Corn Bread

This uses sweet milk and just a touch of sugar. Use either one whole egg or two egg whites.

8-inch square regular or nonstick baking pan
Makes 9 servings

1½ CUPS WHITE CORNMEAL
½ CUP UNBLEACHED ALL-PURPOSE FLOUR
2 TABLESPOONS SUGAR
1 TABLESPOON BAKING POWDER
½ TEASPOON SALT
1¼ CUPS SKIM MILK
¼ CUP CANOLA OIL
1 LARGE EGG, OR 2 LARGE EGG WHITES

1. Preheat the oven to 425°F. Grease an 8-inch square regular pan or use a nonstick baking pan.
2. In a large mixing bowl, stir together the cornmeal, flour, sugar, baking powder and salt. Make a well in the center of the dry ingredients and put in the milk, oil and egg or egg whites. Mix well; beat vigorously for 30 seconds. Pour into the prepared baking pan.
3. Bake in the preheated oven for 25 to 30 minutes, or until the bread begins to pull away from the sides of the pan. Serve warm or cold.

Double Corn Bread

Stir 1 can (7 ounces) whole kernel corn, well-drained, into the batter for Sweet Milk Corn Bread. Bake as before.

Seeded Soda Bread

I always bake my soda breads in a dutch oven. A covered stoneware baker will work just as well.

dutch oven or baking sheet
Makes 1 loaf

4 CUPS UNBLEACHED ALL-PURPOSE FLOUR
1/3 CUP SUGAR
1 TEASPOON BAKING POWDER
1 TEASPOON BAKING SODA
1 TEASPOON SALT
1 TEASPOON CARAWAY SEEDS
1 TEASPOON DILL SEEDS
1 LARGE EGG
1 1/3 CUPS BUTTERMILK
6 TABLESPOONS UNSALTED BUTTER, MELTED AND COOLED

1. Preheat the oven to 450°F. Grease the bottom half of a dutch oven.

2. Use a fork throughout. Stir together the flour, sugar, baking powder, baking soda, salt and seeds in a large bowl. In another bowl, stir together the egg, buttermilk and melted butter. Add the egg mixture to the dry ingredients and stir just until the dough comes together. Turn out onto a lightly floured surface and knead lightly until smooth. Shape into a ball and place in the dutch oven, smooth side up. Cut a cross in the top of the loaf.

3. Cover the dutch oven and place in the preheated oven. Bake for 5 minutes. Reduce the heat to 350°F and bake for 45 to 50 minutes longer, or until golden brown. (The bread can be baked on a greased baking sheet at 350°F for 50 to 60 minutes.) Cool on a wire rack. Serve warm or cold.

Whole Wheat Soda Bread

This is a basic Irish soda bread with a satisfying whole-grain flavor.

dutch oven or baking sheet
Makes 1 loaf

2 CUPS UNBLEACHED ALL-PURPOSE FLOUR
2 CUPS FINELY GROUND OR SIFTED WHOLE WHEAT FLOUR
1 TEASPOON SUGAR
1 TEASPOON SALT
1 TEASPOON BAKING POWDER
1 TEASPOON BAKING SODA
ABOUT 2 CUPS BUTTERMILK

1. Preheat the oven to 375°F. Grease the bottom half of a Dutch oven.

2. Use a fork throughout. In a large mixing bowl, stir together the flours, the sugar, salt, baking powder and baking soda. Add the buttermilk and stir until the dough just comes together. If the dough is dry and crumbly, add extra buttermilk, 1 tablespoon at a time, until the dough comes together. Turn out on a lightly floured surface and knead lightly until smooth. Shape into a ball and place in the dutch oven, smooth side up. Cut a cross in the top of the loaf.

3. Cover the dutch oven and place in the preheated oven. Bake for 50 to 55 minutes, or until golden brown. (The bread can be baked on a greased baking sheet at 375°F for 45 to 50 minutes.) Serve warm or cold.

Olive Oil–Rosemary Biscuits

Here's a two-way biscuit that's packed with flavor. They are flaky when made with the butter, more bread-like without. I don't advise dried rosemary for these. If you can't get fresh rosemary, use parsley instead.

nonstick baking sheet
Makes 12 biscuits

2 CUPS UNBLEACHED ALL-PURPOSE FLOUR
½ TEASPOON SALT
1 TEASPOON FINELY CHOPPED FRESH ROSEMARY LEAVES
1 TABLESPOON BAKING POWDER
2 TABLESPOONS COLD UNSALTED BUTTER, CUT INTO SLIVERS
  (OPTIONAL)
¼ CUP EXTRA-LIGHT OLIVE OIL
⅔ OR ¾ CUP SKIM MILK

1. Preheat the oven to 450°F.
2. Use a fork throughout. Stir together the flour, salt, rosemary and baking powder. Stir in the butter, if using. Stir the olive oil and the milk together (use the smaller amount of milk, if using the butter) and add to the dry ingredients. Stir lightly until the dough just comes together.
3. Toss the dough on a lightly floured surface until no longer sticky. Pat or roll out ½ inch thick. Cut into 2-inch squares. Place on a nonstick baking sheet.
4. Bake the biscuits for 10 to 12 minutes, or until very lightly browned; do not overbake. Serve warm.

Little Butter Biscuits

See Butter-Biscuit Dumplings, page 101.

Nuthin' Muffins

This is a simple basic muffin—easy to whip up anytime. They're good plain or with the addition of raisins or nuts as you wish.

Muffin tin
Makes 12 muffins

2 CUPS UNBLEACHED ALL-PURPOSE FLOUR
1/4 TEASPOON SALT
2 1/2 TEASPOONS BAKING POWDER
1/4 TEASPOON GRATED NUTMEG
1/3 CUP SUGAR
1/3 CUP CANOLA OIL
1 CUP SKIM MILK
1 LARGE EGG

1. Preheat the oven to 375°F. Grease 12 muffin cups or use paper liners.

2. In a mixing bowl, stir together the flour, salt, baking powder, nutmeg and sugar. In a bowl, mix together the oil, milk and egg. Add the liquid ingredients to the dry mixture and mix just until moistened; do not overmix.

3. Divide the batter among the prepared muffin cups. Bake for 20 to 22 minutes, or until lightly browned. Cool on wire racks. Serve warm or cold.

Whole Wheat Muffins

Here's another all-purpose muffin. Nutritious and delicious!

muffin tin
Makes 12 muffins

1 CUP UNBLEACHED ALL-PURPOSE FLOUR
1 CUP FINELY GROUND OR SIFTED WHOLE WHEAT FLOUR

¼ TEASPOON SALT

2 TEASPOONS BAKING POWDER

¼ TEASPOON BAKING SODA

¼ TEASPOON GROUND CINNAMON

¼ TEASPOON GRATED NUTMEG

¼ CUP SUGAR

¼ CUP CANOLA OIL

½ CUP FRESH ORANGE JUICE

½ CUP SKIM MILK

1 LARGE EGG

1. Preheat the oven to 400°F. Grease 12 muffin cups or use paper liners.

2. In a mixing bowl, combine the flours, salt, baking powder, baking soda, cinnamon, nutmeg and sugar. In a bowl, mix together the oil, orange juice, milk and egg. Add the liquid ingredients to the dry mixture and mix just until moistened; do not overmix.

3. Spoon the batter into the prepared muffin cups. Bake for 15 to 18 minutes, or until lightly browned. Cool on wire racks. Serve warm or cold.

Brown Bread Muffins

These are good with any soup or chowder that contains beans. Sometimes I marinate the raisins overnight in 1 to 2 tablespoons rum, adding them to the batter after mixing.

muffin tin
Makes 12 muffins

1 CUP FINELY GROUND OR SIFTED WHOLE WHEAT FLOUR
1 CUP MEDIUM RYE FLOUR
¼ CUP SUGAR
1 TEASPOON BAKING SODA
½ TEASPOON SALT
1 CUP RAISINS
1 CUP BUTTERMILK
¼ CUP CANOLA OIL
¼ CUP MOLASSES
1 LARGE EGG

1. Preheat the oven to 375°F. Grease 12 muffin cups or use paper liners.

2. In a mixing bowl, stir together the flours, sugar, baking soda, salt and raisins. In a bowl, stir together the buttermilk, oil, molasses and egg. Add the liquid ingredients to the dry mixture and mix just until moistened; do not overmix.

3. Spoon the batter into the prepared muffin cups. Bake for 18 to 20 minutes, or until lightly browned. Cool on wire racks. Serve warm or cold.

Beer Batter Muffins

Here's a quick little muffin that's a perfect accompaniment for soups and stews.

regular or nonstick muffin tin
Makes 12 muffins

2¾ CUPS UNBLEACHED ALL-PURPOSE FLOUR

¼ CUP GRATED PARMESAN CHEESE

1 TABLESPOON BAKING POWDER

1 TABLESPOON SUGAR

½ TEASPOON SALT

½ TEASPOON CRACKED BLACK PEPPER

1 CAN (12 OUNCES) BEER

1. Preheat the oven to 375°F. Grease 12 muffin cups, even non-stick. Do not use paper liners.

2. In a mixing bowl, stir together the flour, cheese, baking powder, sugar, salt and pepper. Add the beer and stir just until the dry ingredients are moistened; do not overmix.

3. Spoon the batter into the prepared muffin cups. Bake for about 20 minutes, or until lightly browned. Serve warm or cold.

Buttermilk Crackers

The secret of a good cracker is in rolling out the dough very thin. The desired thickness is about halfway between ¹⁄₁₆ inch and ⅛ inch.

baking sheet
Makes about 12 dozen 2-inch crackers

2 CUPS UNBLEACHED ALL-PURPOSE FLOUR

¼ TEASPOON SALT

¼ TEASPOON BAKING SODA

2 TABLESPOONS CANOLA OIL

¾ CUP BUTTERMILK

1. Use a fork throughout. In a large bowl, stir together the flour, salt and baking soda. Sprinkle the oil over the flour mixture and stir to mix.

Add the buttermilk and stir until the dough comes together. (It may look as though the oil is not evenly distributed; it doesn't matter.)

2. Preheat the oven to 400°F.

3. Work with one-fourth of the dough at a time; cover the remaining dough while you work. Toss the dough on a lightly floured surface until no longer sticky. Press and pat out with your hands to a 6-inch square. Turn the dough over two or three times as you do this, making sure to coat the dough lightly with flour each time it is turned. Roll out to a 12-inch circle or square; the dough should be very thin. Cut into 2-inch squares or diamonds and place close together on an ungreased baking sheet.

4. You can bake the crackers as is, making puffy, blistered crackers. Or, prick each cracker several times with a fork, making them flat. Bake 1 sheet at a time at 400°F for 8 to 10 minutes, or until golden with brown edges. Cool on a wire rack.

5. Continue with the remaining chunks of dough until all of the crackers are baked. Store airtight.

Whole Wheat Crackers

I intended to make a wheat cracker with part white flour, but found myself in my kitchen with only whole wheat flour on the shelf. Being too impatient to wait for the next trip to the store, I decided to experiment and came up with this recipe for a crisp cracker with a wonderful nutty flavor.

nonstick baking sheet
Makes 9 dozen

3 CUPS FINELY GROUND OR SIFTED WHOLE WHEAT FLOUR
1 TEASPOON SALT
½ TEASPOON BAKING SODA
1 PACKAGE ACTIVE DRY YEAST
1 CUP WARM WATER
¼ TEASPOON SUGAR

¼ CUP CANOLA OIL

¼ TEASPOON CIDER VINEGAR

1. In a mixing bowl, combine the flour, salt and baking soda. In a bowl, combine the yeast, warm water and sugar. Let the yeast mixture stand for 5 minutes.

2. Add the yeast mixture to the flour mixture along with the oil and vinegar. Use a wooden spoon to stir the flour into the liquids, until all is incorporated. You may have to use your hands at the end, to get it all mixed. Knead lightly in the bowl.

3. Divide the dough into 3 parts. Form each part into a ball. Cover the dough and let rest for 15 minutes. Meanwhile, preheat the oven to 400°F.

4. Working with one part at a time, roll out the dough on a lightly floured surface to the thickness of cardboard (a little less than ⅛ inch—the thinner you roll them, the crisper they will be). Cut into 1¾-inch squares or circles. Place the cutouts on a nonstick baking sheet, leaving ¼ inch of space between them. Prick the crackers all over with the tines of a fork. Bake for 10 to 12 minutes, or until lightly browned. Cool on wire racks.

5. Continue with the remaining chunks of dough until all of the crackers are baked. Store airtight.

FOOD PROCESSOR TIP: Use the metal blade. Place the flour, salt and baking soda in the workbowl. Pulse to mix. Mix the yeast as before and add to the workbowl along with the oil and the vinegar. Pulse until fairly well mixed. Process just until a ball of dough forms on the blade. Proceed as before.

Home-Style Croutons

These are not dried out for storage like store-bought. Make them fresh for special soups. Croutons are good made with either white or whole-grain breads. They can be plain, with just butter and oil for flavor, or with herbs to complement the soups they accompany. Pair fresh dill or oregano with tomato soup, marjoram or rosemary with chicken, thyme or parsley with beef. If you're a lover of garlic, you can use it with everything.

nonstick baking sheet
Makes 3 cups croutons

6 SLICES OF BREAD, HOMEMADE PREFERRED, CUT ½ INCH THICK
2 TABLESPOONS UNSALTED BUTTER, SOFTENED
1 TABLESPOON EXTRA-VIRGIN OLIVE OIL
½ GARLIC CLOVE, MINCED OR PRESSED (OPTIONAL)
1 TEASPOON CHOPPED FRESH HERBS OF YOUR CHOICE, OR ¼
   TEASPOON DRIED (OPTIONAL)

1. Preheat the oven to 350°F. Leave the crusts on the slices of bread for a rustic appearance. Lay the bread out on a cutting board.

2. In a small bowl, mash together the butter and oil with a fork. Add the garlic and herbs, if using. Spread the mixture on both sides of each slice of bread. Cut into ½-inch dice. Transfer to a nonstick baking sheet.

3. Bake until crisp and golden brown. The time varies with the dryness of the bread; it's best to check every 5 minutes until done. Serve on the side or scattered on top of soup.

For Further Reading

For those who wish to read further about soups, these are a few of my favorite books.

Aaron, Jan. *32 Soups and Stews.* Woodbury, NY: Barron's, 1983.

All Color Book of Soups and Appetizers. New York: Arco, 1984.

Bailey, Lee. *Lee Bailey's Soup Meals: Main Event Soups in Year-Round Menus.* New York: Clarkson N. Potter, 1989.

Better Homes and Gardens Soup and Stews Cook Book. Des Moines, Iowa: Meredith Corporation, 1978.

Betty Crocker's Soups and Stews Cookbook. New York: Golden Press, 1985.

Butel, Jane. *Chili Madness.* New York: Workman Publishing, 1980.

California Culinary Academy Soups and Stews. San Francisco: California Culinary Academy, 1986.

Castle, Coralie. *Soup, Revised Edition.* San Francisco: 101 Productions, 1971, 1981.

Clayton, Bernard, Jr. *The Complete Book of Soups and Stews.* New York: Simon and Schuster, 1984.

Cooking with Bon Appétit, Soups and Salads. Los Angeles: The Knapp Press, 1983.

Cooper, Sandi. *Soups and Salads.* New York: Irena Chalmers Cookbooks, 1982.

Deeming, Sue, and Bill Deeming. *Soups and Sandwiches*. Tucson, AZ: HP Books, 1983.

De Gouy, Louis P. *The Soup Book: 770 Recipes*. New York: Dover Publications, 1949.

Fleischer, Leonore. *The Chicken Soup Book*. New York: Taplinger Publishing, 1977.

Franklin, Rena. *Soups of the Hakafri Restaurant*. Gainesville, FL: Triad Publishing, 1982.

Gerras, Charles, editor. *Rodale's Soups and Salads Cookbook and Kitchen Album*. Emmaus, PA: Rodale Press, 1981.

Gin, Maggie. *One Pot Meals*. Berkeley, CA: 101 Productions, 1976.

Good, Phyllis Pellman, and Rachel Thomas Pellman, editors. *Soups from Amish and Mennonite Kitchens*. Lancaster, PA: Good Books, 1982.

Halpern, Daniel, and Julie Strand. *The Good Food, Soups, Stews and Pastas*. New York: Viking Penguin, 1985.

Hechtlinger, Adelaide. *A Simple Soupbook*. Boston: Branden Press, 1969.

Heriteau, Jacqueline. *A Feast of Soups*. New York: Ballantine Books, 1981, 1982.

Ivens, Dorothy. *Main-Course Soups and Stews*. New York: Harper & Row, 1983.

Janerico, Terence. *The Book of Great Soups, Sandwiches, and Breads*. New York: Van Nostrand Reinhold, 1984.

Lerman, Ann. *Annie Lerman's New Salad and Soup Book*. Philadelphia: Running Press, 1977, 1978, and 1983.

Lockwook, Lu. *Truly Unusual Soups, Second Edition*. Chester, CT: The Globe Pequot Press, 1977, 1983.

Matteson, Marilee, editor. *Small Feasts*. New York: Clarkson N. Potter, 1980.

Maynard, Dave. *Dave Maynard's Soups, Stews and Casseroles*. New York: St. Martin's Press, 1984.

McNair, James K. *James McNair's Soups*. San Francisco: Chronicle Books, 1990.

Migliaccio, Janice Cook. *Follow Your Heart's Vegetarian Soup Cookbook*. Santa Barbara, CA: Woodbridge Press, 1983.

Mitchell, Marge, and Joan Sedgwick. *The Bakery Lane Soup Bowl Cookbook*. New York: Random House, 1976.

Nelson, Kay Shaw. *Stews and Ragouts: Simple and Hearty One-Dish Meals*. New York: Dover Publications, 1974.

One Pot Dishes from the Kitchen of the Rochester Folk Art Guild. Middlesex, NY: Rochester Folk Art Guild, 1975.

Orcutt, Georgia. *Soups, Chowders, and Stews*. Dublin, NH: Yankee Publishing, 1981.

Pappas, Lou Seibert. *Creative Soups and Salads*. Concord, CA: Nitty Gritty Productions, 1983.

Rothschild, Irene. *Cold Soups, Warm Salads*. New York: Dutton, 1990.

The Southern Heritage Soups and Stews Cookbook. Birmingham, AL: Oxmoor House, 1985.

Standard, Stella. *Stella Standard's Soup Book*. New York: Taplinger Publishing, 1978.

Sunset Editors. *Sunset Homemade Soups*. Menlo Park, CA: Lane Publishing, 1985.

Time-Life Editors. *Soups*. Alexandria, VA: Time-Life Books, 1979.

Williamson, Darcy. *The All Natural Soup Cookbook*. Bend, OR: Maverick Publications, 1985.

Index